IMMERSION
Bible Studies
GENESIS

D1506274

Praise for IMMERSION

"This unique Bible study makes Scripture come alive for students. Through the study, students are invited to move beyond the head into the heart of faith."
Bishop Joseph W. Walker, author of *Love and Intimacy*

"If you're looking for a deeper knowledge and understanding of God's Word, you must dive into IMMERSION BIBLE STUDIES. Whether in a group setting or as an individual, you will experience God and his unconditional love for each of us in a whole new way."
Pete Wilson, founding and senior pastor of Cross Point Church

"This beautiful series helps readers become fluent in the words and thoughts of God, for purposes of illumination, strength building, and developing a closer walk with the One who loves us so."
Laurie Beth Jones, author of *Jesus, CEO and The Path*

"I highly commend to you IMMERSION BIBLE STUDIES, which tells us what the Bible teaches and how to apply it personally."
John Ed Mathison, author of *Treasures of the Transformed Life*

"The IMMERSION BIBLE STUDIES series is no less than a game changer. It ignites the purpose and power of Scripture by showing us how to do more than just know God or love God; it gives us the tools to love like God as well."
Shane Stanford, author of *You Can't Do Everything . . . So Do Something*

IMMERSION
Bible Studies
GENESIS

J. Ellsworth Kalas

Abingdon Press

Nashville

GENESIS
IMMERSION BIBLE STUDIES
by J. Ellsworth Kalas

Copyright © 2011 by Abingdon Press

Library of Congress Cataloging-in-Publication Data

Kalas, J. Ellsworth, 1923-
  Genesis / J. Ellsworth Kalas.
    p. cm. — (Immersion Bible studies)
  ISBN 978-1-4267-1623-2 (curriculum — printed text plus -cover : alk. paper) 1. Bible. O.T. Genesis—Textbooks. I. Title.
  BS1239.K35 2011
  222'.11007—dc22

                                                                              2011010879

Editor: Jack A. Keller, Jr.
Leader Guide Writer: John P. "Jack" Gilbert

11 12 13 14 15 16 17 18 19 20—10 9 8 7 6 5 4 3 2 1

Manufactured in the United States of America

Contents

REVIEW TEAM

IMMERSION BIBLE STUDIES

*A fresh new look at the Bible, from beginning to end,
and what it means in your life.*

Welcome to IMMERSION!

We've asked some of the leading Bible scholars, teachers, and pastors to help us with a new kind of Bible study. IMMERSION remains true to Scripture but always asks, "Where are you in your life? What do you struggle with? What makes you rejoice?" Then it helps you read the Scriptures to discover their deep, abiding truths. IMMERSION is about God and God's Word, and it is also about you—not just your thoughts, but your feelings and your faith.

In each study you will prayerfully read the Scripture and reflect on it. Then you will engage it in three ways:

Claim Your Story
Through stories and questions, think about your life, with its struggles and joys.

Enter the Bible Story
Explore Scripture and consider what God is saying to you.

Live the Story
Reflect on what you have discovered, and put it into practice in your life.

IMMERSION makes use of an exciting new translation of Scripture, the Common English Bible (CEB). The CEB and IMMERSION BIBLE STUDIES will offer adults:

- the emotional expectation to find the love of God
- the rational expectation to find the knowledge of God
- reliable, genuine, and credible power to transform lives
- clarity of language

Whether you are using the Common English Bible or another translation, IMMERSION BIBLE STUDIES will offer a refreshing plunge into God's Word, your life, and your life with God.

1.

How It All Began

Genesis 1–2

Claim Your Story

Isaac Bashevis Singer is known to many of us as a winner of the Nobel Prize in Literature (1978). He knew himself, however, as a son and grandson of rabbis, for whom learning the Book of Genesis "was the greatest event in my life."[1] But he recalls that even as a boy, he began dealing with problems he found in the opening chapters of Genesis—questions about time, space, eternity, infinity. How can something be created from nothing? And how do these questions relate to modern learning?

As you read Singer's questions, you probably realize that you had some of these same questions as a child and that some have remained with you as a youth or an adult.

As Christians reading Genesis, we also wonder how this ancient book relates to the New Testament and to our Christian faith as a whole. Especially, you and I ask what Genesis says to us personally. This is a proper question because the Bible is never simply a source of detached knowledge; it is a call to a new, real, and profound way of life, a life that recognizes that its goal is in its relationship with God. As such, the Bible speaks to us personally. It finds its way into the soul and marrow of our being. No book does this more incisively than the Book of Genesis.

So, of course, you have questions as you read Genesis because Genesis goes into the heart of life and its purposes. It is by way of your questions that you will come to a greater knowledge of the Scriptures and of life itself. In the process, you will come to a deeper and more challenging faith in God.

Enter the Bible Story

Since planet Earth is the only home I've known thus far, I'm sentimental about it and like to think of it as favorably as possible. Genesis reports that when God began the Creation process, "the earth was without shape or form" (1:2). Robert Alter translates the Hebrew as "welter and waste."[2] The prevailing mood at this early point in Earth's story was not light and promise; rather, "it was dark over the deep sea" (1:2). From this kind of language we might conclude that God was beginning a reclamation project. In a way, it's an appropriate introduction to all that will follow in the grand Bible story. All of God's loving investment in us human beings unfolds in settings of "welter and waste."

We feel reassured, therefore, when we're told that "God's wind swept over the waters" (Genesis 1:2). We feel all the better about that wind from God when we remember that in the Hebrew the same word can be translated either *wind, breath,* or *spirit.* Thus the King James Version says that "the Spirit of God moved upon the face of the waters." Whichever word is used, the action is from God.

Order and Light Out of Welter and Waste

I feel better with each continuing step in the Creation process. I'm glad that God's first command was, "Let there be light" (Genesis 1:3). Something in our human soul abhors darkness, whether it be physical,

---

About the Scripture

What's in a Word?

Genesis gets its name from the Greek word meaning "origin." It is an apt title because in Genesis we read of the origins of the universe, of humans, of social order beginning with the family, of sin, of crime, of farming, and of urban life—and from a Christian point of view, as we shall see later, the origin of salvation.

In the Hebrew Bible this book is entitled *Bereshith,* meaning "in the beginning," which in the Hebrew is the opening word of Genesis.

intellectual, emotional, or spiritual. We long for light. And I'm also happy for the *method* by which God created. It was by the communing action of speech. Mind you, I honor God as the ultimate engineer, the supreme craftsperson, and the complete landscape architect. But I'm glad that Genesis tells us that the Creator *talked* with the stuff that was going into our human home. I feel better about this dwelling place of earth and water and trees and sky when I understand that it happened with some kind of eternal conversation. And I like it that at every pause in the story we're told that "God saw how good [each thing] was" and that at the completion, God felt "it was supremely good" (Genesis 1:31). I like living in a world that gave God pleasure in its creating and that was finished with a divine stamp of approval.

Yet while this pleases me, it also puts a burden on me. This lovely world is a divine trust. If I have any true reverence for God the Creator, I will do nothing to harm this earth and everything possible to preserve, bless, and develop it.

I'm fascinated by the way Genesis describes Creation in a day-by-day way. It pictures an orderly God. Whatever may have been the "welter and waste" with which the process began, the Creator knew how to bring beauty and perfection out of it, with no intervals of confusion and no need to work overtime. It is always "evening and . . . morning," a good day's work. At its completion, the work was celebrated by a day of rest. "God blessed the seventh day and made it holy, because on it God rested from all the work of creation" (Genesis 2:3). Work is essential to our planet and to us humans who are made in the Creator's image. But rest is also essential; and when we ignore this need for rest, we not only violate the way we are made, we also deny ourselves the exquisite joy of a task completed. By the nature of some work, a task is not done and we know that we'll have to pick it up again another day. To rest is an act of trust, a declaration that our work is good and that if we put it aside in holy rest, we will resume work responsibilities better on the day after our sabbath.

Holy is the key word in what I have just said. The seventh-day principle in the Creation story is significantly more than sociological,

Across the Testaments

The Sabbath

According to Professor Andrew Louth, "The early chapters of Genesis had arguably a greater influence on the development of Christian theology than did any other part of the Old Testament."[3] When we read the opening words of Genesis (especially in the language of the King James Version), we realize that we hear those words echoed in the opening words of the Gospel of John. As Genesis tells us about the birth of the sabbath day, we understand better why Judaism's leaders repeatedly made such an issue of sabbath observance in their controversies with Jesus.

economic, or philosophical issues, though all these elements are present; it is a spiritual fact. "*God* blessed the seventh day and *made it holy.*"

Obviously, I must pause at this point in the Genesis story to deal with a question that inevitably comes to many minds, especially in our contemporary culture: Is the Genesis story scientifically correct? In a sense this is like asking if a Bach cantata was a good football game. Science seeks, rightly, to explain *how*; Genesis talks about *who*. The Genesis story is concerned about the *Who* (Creator) and the *who* (humanity)—the God who created and the humans responsible to care for the creation. As a believer, I am satisfied that God was behind the creative process, whatever the factors by which it may have taken place. I love the Genesis story because I understand poetry better than I understand molecules, but I honor the work of the scientist who searches for more knowledge of the *how*. Personally, I feel that a scientist who eliminates God from the Creation story has gotten beyond the realm of science, just as I, a believer, am likely to get beyond the realm of faith when I try to offer too many "how" details.

The Unique Role of Human Beings

Human beings don't appear in the Creation story until near the end of the first chapter of Genesis, but our entry is auspicious. When we're told that "God created humanity in God's own image" (Genesis 1:27), we know that we humans have a unique role in the story that will follow. We get a further insight into our human nature in a second account of human creation that serves as a kind of philosophical reprise on the first. It is both playful and powerful, with stuff enough for ten thousand poems and a million late night discussions: "The LORD God formed the human from the topsoil of the fertile land and blew life's breath into his nostrils. The human came to life" (2:7).

This human creature was made of the dust of the earth, but the breath within was the breath of God. We are, as I like to phrase it, "a bit of sod and a breath from God." We are as common as the earth on which we walk, yet we are dramatically distinctive from all the rest of creation because the life that is in us is an investment from the very person of God. This infers a peculiar sacredness in human life, a fact that ought to inform the respect we have for ourselves and for all human creatures. We humans tend to judge one another on a variety of matters—race, sex, ethnicity, intelligence, wealth, achievement, personality, physical attractiveness, or prowess. But as Genesis sees it, nothing is so basic or so ultimate about us as this: God crafted us in God's own image, and the breath within us is God's investment. This, above all other measures and considerations, is who we are.

As such, God entrusts creation to us. "Take charge of the fish of the sea, the birds of the sky, and everything crawling on the ground" (Genesis 1:28). We're given an Eden, "to farm it and to take care of it" (2:15). Of all the innumerable species on this planet, it appears that we are the only ones who can bless or curse it, benefit or exploit it. Thus the welfare of all

---

Across the Testaments

Christ and Adam

The New Testament speaks of Christ as the second Adam. "So it is also written, The first human, Adam, became a living person, and the last Adam became a spirit that gives life. . . . The first human was from the earth made from dust; the second human is from heaven" (1 Corinthians 15:45, 47). Thus the first Christians saw our human race under the curse of death by Adam's sin but given eternal life through the death and resurrection of Christ.

the other species rests on us. If we don't show regard for the rest of the planet's inhabitants, whether flower, fauna, or human being, we will some-day find our planet home a desolate place.

We humans have another particular quality in us: We are creatures with the power of choice. Long before there were systems of government, centuries before anyone imagined such instruments as citizenship and elections, we became voters. The choice was between good and evil, and it was offered in a setting of beneficence: "Eat your fill from all of the garden's trees; but don't eat from the tree of the knowledge of good and evil, because on the day you eat from it, you will die!" (Genesis 2:16-17). We humans are surrounded by benefits, but there is one place that spells trouble—big trouble! It's interesting to see how attractive that singularly forbidden place becomes.

Created for Relationship

At this point the scene is almost idyllic. The home plot is called *Eden, Paradise*. At each stage of Creation, God has found it good and then in conclusion, *extremely good*. But now we hear a *"not good."* "It's not good that the human is alone. I will make him a helper that is perfect for him" (Genesis 2:18). However perfect the setting, however ideal the weather, however beautiful the scenery, the perfection is incomplete until it is shared. Even the good is not good; it is unfinished and unfulfilled until someone shares it with us.

Some of us love solitude, perhaps even to the point where we desire it more than we desire company. But into our solitude we take a book which, of course, came from another person; or we take music, which carries the emotion of another person. Nothing argues more convincingly against selfishness than the Genesis story with its insistence that paradise requires other persons. We're made that way. So John Donne the poet-preacher wrote, "No man is an Island, entire of it self; every man is a piece of the Continent . . .; any man's death diminishes me, because I am involved in Mankind."[4]

"So the LORD God put the human into a deep and heavy sleep, and took one of his ribs and closed up the flesh over it. With the rib taken from the human, the Lᴏʀᴅ God fashioned a woman and brought her to the human being. The human said,

> 'This one finally is bone from my bones
> and flesh from my flesh.
> She will be called a woman
> because from a man she was taken.'" (Genesis 2:21-23).

When I read this passage, I remember the novelist who explained repeatedly that some truths are too big to be conveyed as facts or data; they can only be understood as symbols or word-pictures. I know of no psychological or sociological study that can explain our human need for another as poignantly as this Genesis story. There is in every human being a missing rib. All of us are incomplete. Never is our incompleteness more ironic than when, in a fit of independence, we announce our sufficiency. Even such an announcement needs an audience or it is wasted.

The Genesis writer goes on to endorse the institution of marriage. "This is the reason that a man leaves his father and mother and embraces his wife, and they become one flesh" (Genesis 2:24). A sense of loyalty might make humans feel they should never leave home; we might think that the parents who have reared us now have a right to our continued presence and service. But Genesis tells us that life must go on and that though we owe much to our parents, we also are debtors to generations to come. So we are not violating our obligation to parents when we leave; we are carrying the obligation into generations to come.

Across the Testaments
Marriage as a Symbol

Genesis 2 gives a high view of marriage. Ephesians 5:25-32 uses this elevated thinking to describe Christ's relationship to the church as that of groom to bride, an analogy that is emphasized even more dramatically in the Book of Revelation (19:6-8). So the message unfolds, quite literally from Genesis to Revelation.

Genesis is also altogether candid and unembarrassed about the nature of marriage. It is not simply an economic, social, or spiritual union; it is also physical. Indeed, it is this physical quality that especially identifies it. Many other relationships are also social, economic, or spiritual; but marriage is defined by our becoming "one *flesh*." Genesis makes the point emphatically. "The two of them were naked, the man and his wife, but they weren't embarrassed" (2:25). There is nothing titillating or suggestive about this description; rather, it is quite matter-of-fact. This, Genesis tells us, is the way it is.

Live the Story

The questions we first ask as children are likely to be life's big questions. As we grow older, we may amend the form of these questions and seek to phrase them in more sophisticated language; but the early questions tend to deal with the basic stuff of life. These are the questions that Genesis raises and then answers. But Genesis leaves much to faith. This shouldn't surprise us because the ultimate question in Genesis is whether we will believe the commands and promises of God, as we shall see in the next chapter of this study.

But Genesis speaks to you and me as it tells us what God is like: a God who loves creation and delights in sharing it with us humans and the other inhabitants of our planet, a God who is the ultimate craftsperson but who chooses to "talk" the creation into existence, showing us that the Creator is above all a communicator. If that be so, what does God expect of you and me? As persons made in the divine image, our first calling and privilege is the act of communing with God and then with our fellow human creatures.

Genesis also tells us that we humans are the caretakers of this planet and its awesome resources. How do you and I do justice to this stewardship? This is a question I answer every day—and you do, too, whether we realize it or not.

Since God has made us to need fellow humans and to be needed by them, how do you and I live in a way that blesses other persons and allows other persons to bless us?

Do you know God better after reading the first two chapters of Genesis? I hope so. But you and I have only just begun. Is there something in you that wants passionately to know God and to know yourself and others still more deeply and caringly? I think this is something of what Isaac Bashevis Singer had in mind when he concluded his essay on Genesis, "No matter how the human brain might grow, it will always come back to the idea that God has created heaven and earth, man and animals, with a will and a plan, and that, despite all the evil life undergoes, there is a purpose in Creation and eternal wisdom."[5] Whatever our questions, we continue to return to Genesis because here we find purpose and wisdom.

1 From "Genesis," by Isaac Bashevis Singer, in *Congregation: Contemporary Writers Read the Jewish Bible*, edited by David Rosenberg (Harcourt Brace Jovanovich, 1987); page 3.

2 From *The Five Books of Moses*, by Robert Alter (W.W. Norton, 2004); page 17.

3 From *Ancient Christian Commentary on Scripture: Old Testament*, edited by Andrew Louth (InterVarsity Press, 2001); Vol. I, page xxxix.

4 From *Devotions Upon Emergent Occasions*, "Meditation XVII," by John Donne, in *The Oxford Dictionary of Quotations*, edited by Elizabeth Knowles (Oxford University Press, 2004); page 282.

5 From "Genesis," by Isaac Bashevis Singer, in *Congregation: Contemporary Writers Read the Jewish Bible*; page 8.

2.

The Beginnings of Sin and of Grace

Genesis 3:1–4:17, 25

Claim Your Story

If you have ever watched the television game show *Who Wants to Be a Millionaire?* you probably know that it ran for several years in prime time and that it is now purportedly the most internationally popular TV franchise of all time, having aired in some 100 countries. Contestants on the show, when faced with a difficult question, were allowed to use the "50-50 Lifeline," which eliminated two of the four multiple-choice answers. Theoretically, that made it easier for contestants to choose the right answer. In actuality though, a choice remained between two seemingly plausible answers.

This phenomenon is standard procedure in many multiple-choice exams. Test makers deliberately make one of the incorrect answers especially attractive in order to make sheer guesswork unsuccessful. The appealing incorrect answer is sometimes called the "attractive distracter."

We humans have perennially faced various types of real-life attractive distracters. No doubt you have faced some yourself. What have been the attractive distracters in your life, the tantalizing options that seemed good at the time but ultimately proved not to be the best? What was it that led you astray? What were the consequences? When you look around your world, what evidence do you see that other people are likewise making choices that are out of sync with God's best intention?

The biblical Book of Genesis tells the story not simply of Adam and Eve, but of you and me—people who succumbed to an attractive distracter with serious consequences. Let's take a closer look.

Enter the Bible Story

You and I learned as long ago as our first hearings of the tales of Little Red Riding Hood or The Three Little Pigs that every story has its villain. That's because life as we've experienced it always seems to have its villains. Sometimes, however, it's hard to recognize the villain; and that's where our problems become more complicated.

A stranger enters the biblical story in Genesis 3: a snake, "the most intelligent of all the wild animals that the LORD God had made" (3:1). This snake would therefore seem the best ally for the man and the woman. But Robert Alter's translation describes the snake as "the most *cunning*,"[1] and that word suggests that the snake's intelligence was devoted to deception. The snake raised a question, one having to do with belief, and addressed the question to the woman. "Did God really say that you shouldn't eat from any tree in the garden?" (3:1). The woman replied correctly that God had made all of the fruit of the garden available except for the fruit of the tree "in the middle of the garden"; of that tree God said, "Don't eat from it, and don't touch it, or you will die" (3:3).

It's significant that the tree is in "the middle of the garden." This tree is the issue in the garden, around which the garden's very existence as a garden depends. Relate to the tree properly, and the garden remains Eden; violate it, and Eden is lost.

The snake contradicted what God said. "You won't die!" (Genesis 3:4). More than that, the snake raised a question about the character of God—that God was jealous of the potential in the man and the woman, knowing that if they ate of this tree, they would "see clearly"; and they would "be like God, knowing good and evil" (3:5). The case was persuasive enough that the woman did some further research on her own. Her research had nothing to do with the claims the serpent had made, but she did find that the tree was "beautiful with delicious food and that the tree would provide wisdom" (3:6). She not only ate from the tree herself, she also gave some to her husband, who also ate.

The woman knew what God had said, and she seemed to understand it; but she opened herself to confusion by listening to the intruder. When he told her that she would become like God, she forgot that she and the man were already made in the image of God and possessed of God's life-breath. One wonders especially why she wanted to know "good and evil." What is it about this knowledge that is so appealing? And how is it that this is still the issue above all others? No wonder that America's iconic novelist John Steinbeck insisted that there is actually only one story, the story of good and evil, and how that story works itself out in our individual lives.

The ultimate decision made by the woman and man was the decision of *belief*. They chose to believe the intruder rather than to believe their Creator. To put it still more starkly, they trusted the word of a stranger over the word and deeds of the God who made them. There need be no speculation as to the nature of the first sin. It was the sin of disobedience, springing from the sin of disbelief, that is, to believe in something other than God.

Consequences of Human Disobedience

The woman and the man had no idea, of course, what they would get when they sought this knowledge of good and evil. Their first reaction was to become conscious—painfully so!—of their nakedness. We're inclined to interpret this experience as a recognition of their sexuality. Sexuality was probably a factor, but far more was involved. The man and woman had come to see themselves in a new light, and they made fig leaf garments to hide themselves—not so much from each other as from themselves. It's interesting that we still use the language of their experience to describe our feelings when we have told another person something that we had previously kept hidden or when we have an inner experience where we see ourselves more clearly. "I felt as if I were stark naked," we say, just like the man and the woman in Eden.

So now they hid, by way of their fig leaf garments. Then when they heard "the sound of the LORD God walking in the garden" at the time of "that day's cool evening breeze," they hid themselves "from the LORD God in the middle of the garden's trees" (Genesis 3:8). The garden's stewards were now fugitives from the garden's Owner. The romanticist in me likes to think that the innate loneliness we so easily feel in the "gloaming hour" of early evening is our soul's hunger for the closeness of God we knew in Eden, that is, the perfection of communion with God that God desires for us and for which our human souls unceasingly long.

The meeting with God was not pleasant. God called the man: "Where are you?" (Genesis 3:9). This is the basic theological question, the inquiry into our soul's whereabouts. In a sense it is the question of the counselor to the client. We have to identify where we are before we can begin relocating. It is also the essence of the call to repentance. We have to declare our present spiritual location—that is, our sin—so we can begin the process of turning around and taking a new course.

Unfortunately, the man and the woman responded as we humans so often do. The man blamed the woman (and indirectly, God: "the woman *you* gave me" [Genesis 3:12]), and the woman blamed the serpent. This is the second sin: our unwillingness to accept responsibility for what we have done. In some ways it is even worse than the first sin because it keeps us from dealing redemptively with the first sin.[2] A common proverb that goes back to at least the late sixteenth century declares that "to err is human." But to have the good sense to acknowledge our errors—our sins!—and to seek to change is to see humanity at its highest potential because it is in such self-recognition and vulnerability that we are ready to be born again. To put it in the language of the Creation picture, "To err is the stuff of the clay from which we're made; to repent is to exercise the breath of God that is in us."

Sin and the Next Generation

Both Adam and Eve carried something of Eden with them into the world "east of Eden." Our culture would call it *optimism*; the Bible calls it *hope*. Adam showed it when he named the woman "Eve," a word that in the Hebrew sounds like *life* or *live*. He called her that, Genesis says, "because she is the mother of everyone who lives" (Genesis 3:20). I like the man's hope. After all, he might have identified the woman with death, since she seemed to have opened the door to death by her visit with the serpent. Instead he saw her as the life-giver.

As for the woman, she showed her hope when she named her first-born "Cain," a name that in the Hebrew conveyed her conviction, "I have given life to a man with the LORD's help" (Genesis 4:1). I am impressed by Eve's sense of partnership with God. She saw her role as a divine assignment, carrying on God's breath of life. More than that, I hear her hope. She saw this child as the one who would strike the head of the serpent. By contrast, no special significance is given in the name of the second son, "Abel"; indeed, he is simply "Cain's brother" (4:2).

Admirable as was the couple's hope, I suspect we will have to recognize it as naïve. The pure in heart are often seen by every generation as being naïve. Not so. In truth, the naïve are really those who don't recognize the subtlety of sin and its far-reaching impact. Thus when the financial or sexual misconduct of a public figure is revealed, the person will often speak of the "mistake" he or she has made, as if it were a misspelled word on a test, and often seem surprised at the extent of the consequences. We're very naïve about sin, just like our ancient ancestors.

Tragically, Cain (the first son and the expected carrier of hope) proved instead to be just the opposite. He became the first murderer; and what's worse, the victim was his blood brother. It is as if Cain becomes the transmitter of the judgment carried in God's warning to Adam: "On the day you eat from it [the tree], you will die!" (Genesis 2:17). The spiritual quality of death showed itself in alienation from God, which came immediately; but the physical quality of death appeared in Cain's killing of Abel. Sin destroys not only the perpetrator; it does violence to all of life. Sin always has a second generation. Because we belong to this human race, we cannot live or die simply to ourselves. If we are good, there comes from us a fallout of goodness; and if we are evil, we inevitably bring pain to others. So as Adam and Eve leave the garden, we can say to their descendants, "Watch out!"

The high irony of Cain's sin is that it began at such a relatively innocent level, jealousy, and in such an unlikely setting, worship. Cain and

Across the Testaments

The Essence of True Worship

When the woman of Samaria dialogued with Jesus about worship, she was concerned about the proper *place*: "Our ancestors worshipped on this mountain, but you and your people say that it is necessary to worship in Jerusalem" (John 4:20). Jesus immediately explained that God was seeking a people who would "worship in spirit and truth" (4:23-24). Jesus could have illustrated his point with the story of Cain and Abel. Both men brought what they had; but Cain's spirit was wrong, as demonstrated by the way he responded to God. He was not worshiping God but seeking favor, which means that his worship was self-directed and thus was not "true."

Abel were young agricultural entrepreneurs. Cain was a farmer, and Abel was a rancher. The day came when they presented their offerings to God. Each gave a product of his labor, Cain "from the land's crops" and Abel from "his flock's oldest offspring with their fat" (Genesis 4:3-4). God looked favorably on Abel's gift but not on Cain's. This made Cain very angry; he "looked resentful" (4:5).

Now if Cain had been wise, he would have asked Abel how it was that he had pleased God; but we rarely do wise things when we're angry. It also seems to me that Cain was suffering from the problem his parents had: He wanted a shortcut to godliness. Then, instead of seeking true help, he decided to get rid of his competition. Cain led his brother out to the field, away from interference; and there he killed him. When God confronted Cain with the question, "Where is your brother Abel?" (Genesis 4:9a), Cain answered with what has become a classic line in sociology, economics, politics, and basic daily living: "Am I my brother's keeper?" (4:9b, NRSV). The answer is now as it has always been: Yes.

God replied, "The voice of your brother's blood is crying to me from the ground" (Genesis 4:10). The ground was now cursed for Cain; and he was a fugitive, "a roving nomad on the earth" (4:12). Cain responded as all us sinners do: He feared that everyone else was just like him, so therefore someone would soon kill him. But God put a mark on Cain, to protect his life. In time, Cain married and had a son. Cain built a city and named it after his son. Thus he tried to give his son what he himself had lost: a permanent home in a social setting. The vagabond wanted his son to be a settled citizen.

Faith and Grace

Let me note several matters in this unfolding story. A question: Why did God favor Abel's sacrifice over Cain's? The New Testament Book of Hebrews answers, "By faith Abel offered a better sacrifice to God than Cain" (Hebrews 11:4). Genesis hints when it tells us that Abel gave of "his flock's oldest offspring with their fat" (4:4). Giving the firstborn and the fat was a recognition of God's primacy in Abel's life. We see Cain's lack in his response to God. Instead of seeking to remedy his shortcoming (that is, repenting), he "became very angry" (4:5). The ultimate issue in all worship is *attitude*—not amount, not form or ritual, not eloquence or excellence of performance, but attitude.

Also, we shouldn't leave this chapter without seeing grace at work. Sin is such a prominent issue in Genesis 3 and 4 that we're likely to miss the beautiful and more significant fact of grace.

Grace appeared first in God's calling the man and woman. God could justifiably have discarded them, or at least have waited for them to turn Godward. Instead, God declared that the seed of the woman would "strike" the serpent's head (Genesis 3:15), which was an assurance that in spite of her sin, the woman would have the last word in her relationship to her adversary, the serpent. Third, rather than abandoning the man and woman, God graciously dressed them in leather clothes—surely better

---

About the Christian Faith

What It Is to Be Human

Christianity has a high view of us humans. It teaches that we are free to choose and therefore are responsible. We are influenced by heredity and environment, but we are not controlled by them. In practice our culture feels that our genetic code is our demon and that we are helpless in dealing with it. God says to us, as to Cain, "You must rule over it" (Genesis 4:7). The Christian faith teaches that grace will empower us to do so.

protection than fig leaves that wither and crumble. Fourth, when Cain grew angry at the altar, God reasoned with him: "If you do the right thing, won't you be accepted?" (Genesis 4:7a). Still more, God assured Cain that he could win the soul's battle: "It will entice you, but you must rule over it" (4:7c).

And there was still more grace. In a tragic sense, Adam and Eve had lost both their sons—Abel by murder and Cain by alienation and expulsion. It looked as if all their dreams were gone. But Eve gave birth to another child. With holy insight she named him "Seth 'because God has given me another child in place of Abel whom Cain killed.' " (Genesis 4:25). We humans are foolish; we humans are sinful. But God is gracious.

Live the Story

The more we read the third and fourth chapters of Genesis, the more we realize that we're reading our own story. Like Adam and Eve, you and I have our own ideas about what is most valuable and who or what we are going to trust. You and I can see that things aren't the way they are supposed to be; yet, like Adam and Eve and Cain, we are prone to ignore or deny our responsibility for what we as individuals or members of groups do that is contrary to God's purposes. That's the bad news.

The good news is that God still cares. Genesis tells us not only that God cares but also that God initiates the solution to our problems and pursues us (as was the case with Adam and Eve and Cain) to help us solve those problems.

But you and I still have to make decisions. Sin "will entice you, but you must rule over it" (Genesis 4:7c). This is the agony and the ecstasy of being human. We have the capacity to dream and to destroy dreams—for ourselves and for others. We can be saints, or we can be scoundrels. And while it is true that sin "will entice" us, *grace* also entices us, and in tones of divine love.

So here's the question for you and me, a question that calls for personal reflection about the choices we make: When have you been following God's direction, and when have you been pursuing attractive distracters? Are there places in your life where you need to take responsibility for a poor choice? What can you do to get back on the right path? Are you able to embrace as your own the biblical truth that God never has given up on you and never will?

1 From *The Five Books of Moses*, by Robert Alter (W.W. Norton, 2004); page 24.
2 From *Old Testament Stories from the Back Side*, by J. Ellsworth Kalas (Abingdon Press, 1995); pages 13–21.

3.

The Flood: Judgment and Promise

Genesis 4:18–9:29

Claim Your Story

We might conclude that when Cain killed his brother Abel, the human story had gotten as bad as it could get. What could be worse than for a person to kill a sibling—and after a time of worship at that! But at least Cain tried to hide his crime. One of his descendants, Lamech, committed murder, then boasted about it in a poem he composed for his wives (Genesis 4:23-24). When we boast of our evil rather than being shamed by it, human depravity has found a most desolate place.

Yet it could be worse. Cain and Lamech make headlines because their evil is so out of the ordinary. But what if corrupt conduct is so commonplace that it no longer draws headlines? What if evil becomes the norm, so that nothing shocks us? If sin becomes average, is there any future for righteousness?

Does God care? Or is the character of God so righteous that it cannot endure pervasive evil? Is there such a thing as the judgment of God? If so, is its quality of judgment one of mercy or of anger?

These are questions we face in the monumental story of the great flood and of one person who made a difference, a man named Noah. As we read this story, we should ponder other periods of human history when evil seemed especially gross. Then, reflectively, we should ask ourselves how it is in our time, our century, our world, and how, in turn, we should respond to the culture in which we live.

Enter the Bible Story

The fourth chapter of Genesis ends with a burst of light. Not only does the story have a new beginning with the birth of Seth—a "child in place of Abel," as Eve saw it (Genesis 4:25)—but the Genesis writer also tells us that after the birth of Seth's first child, "at that time, people began to worship in the LORD's name" (4:26). It was a time of spiritual renewal, regaining something of the relationship with God that had characterized Eden, humanity's highest vision.

Then ordinariness set in. Religious renewal, the reality of "the LORD's name," is powerful and exhilarating; but even the greatest realities must be carefully tended, or they will be lost in the routine of life.

So it is that we go from the last line of Genesis 4, with a renewal of true worship, to the astonishing announcement of Genesis 6:5: "The LORD saw that humanity had become thoroughly evil on the earth and that every idea their minds thought up was always completely evil."

How Is It That Evil Asserts Itself?

How is it that the high resolves of January 1 become forgotten thoughts by early February? What happens to a church between the day it celebrates a visionary "purpose statement" and when the statement is nothing more than a forgotten line on the bulletin cover? And how is it that the exuberance of a wedding day settles into a tired friendship, with more emphasis on *tired* than on *friendship*?

Genesis 5 may have more significance than we think. It is a stylized obituary column, giving us nothing more than name, age at the time of the birth of the first child, then the number of years the person lived, until we read, "and he died." Even the extraordinary number of years seems to give a kind of tedium to the story; as your neighbor says after reporting a day of petty happenings, "But life does go on!"

The only exception in the obituary report is Enoch. His story is different. "Enoch walked with God and disappeared because God took him" (Genesis 5:24). Enoch did what his ancestors had started to do in Genesis 4:26, and he did it with such excellence that his life demonstrated a unique communion with God until that communion absorbed his entire being. And Enoch did it because in the midst of ordinariness he did a daily kind of thing, a *pedestrian* kind of thing, if you'll excuse the pun: He *walked* with God.

But the most unsettling part of the human story as it unfolds in Genesis is that the people described in Genesis 6:5 as "thoroughly evil" were not only the descendants of Cain and Lamech, they included the descendants of the line of Seth. They came also from the line that we thought would be humanity's redeeming element.

A Person for the Times

I'm uneasy when people describe situations or times with words like *the worst* or *the best*. I suspect that in general we're wiser to use Charles Dickens' classic line, "It was the best of times, it was the worst of times."[1] That is, life usually is pretty much a mix of the good and the bad.

But the writer of Genesis had a specific measure in mind. Humankind, Genesis tells us, had become so thoroughly evil "that every idea their minds thought up was always completely evil" (6:5). It is not only that persons were doing wicked things; their minds were absorbed in corruption. A community or a political system can pass laws to correct or control specific deeds, but who can rein in the thoughts of the human mind? If all thought is evil, any effort to bring evil under control is useless; the vile mind will simply find another monstrous way to exercise its shame. And if the mind is filled to the brim with evil, there's no room for a good or redemptive thought to assert itself. In other words, the Scripture is telling us that the moral scene was altogether out of control. In a word, it was hopeless.

It was so hopeless, in fact, that Genesis gives the ultimate diagnosis. As God looked at the scene, we are introduced to the divine broken heart. "I regret I ever made them" (Genesis 6:7).

I'm glad the story doesn't end there. The Genesis account continues, "But as for Noah, the LORD approved of him. . . . In his generation, Noah was a moral and exemplary man; he walked with God" (Genesis 6:8-9).

Noah and the Last Days

When questioned about the last days, Jesus answered, "As it was in the time of Noah, so it will be at the coming of the Human One. In those days before the flood, people were eating and drinking, marrying and giving in marriage, until the day Noah entered the ark. They didn't know what was happening until the flood came and swept them all away" (Matthew 24:37-39). So it will be, Jesus said, at the time of his return. Most people will be absorbed in their usual pursuits, oblivious to the judgment that is coming.

I'm fascinated that the biblical writer uses the same phrase to describe Noah as he used earlier to describe Enoch: He "walked with God" (5:22, 24). In Enoch's case, the next line is that he "disappeared because God took him" (5:24). We could summarize Noah's story by continuing, "He stuck around because God used him." I can't tell you how my spirits are lifted by the sentence, "In his generation, Noah was a moral and exemplary man" (6:9). The times were inconceivably bad. Not only was conduct evil beyond description, the human mind was working overtime to find new levels of degradation. Yet in that very generation, Noah appeared. Those of us with a godly conscience work to establish a culture in which goodness will prosper and grow. But sometimes all our best efforts fail, and the times are evil. At such times God brings a grand soul out of the most hopeless circumstances, like a rose in a city dump.

We ask ourselves how this can be. Probably somewhere a historian or a sociologist has developed a theory. I take hope in a conviction taught by the Holy Scriptures, that is, God is involved in our human story. Scripture insists that God has more at stake in our history than we do. Thus time and again, even in generations most desolate, there is a Noah.

The biblical writers are sparing when they describe their characters. Thus Abraham is "God's friend" (James 2:23), and David is "a man after [God's] own heart" (1 Samuel 13:14, NRSV), and Job is "blameless and upright" (Job 1:1, NRSV). Like master novelists, historians, or biographers, the biblical writers tell us what the person did and leave it to us to find adequate adjectives.

Noah "walked with God" (Genesis 6:9). He listened; so when God said, "Make a wooden ark" (6:14), he began building. The details were in broad strokes; this ark was not going to be a luxury liner but a place of survival. God warned Noah but also reassured him: "Everything on earth is about to take its last breath. But I will set up my covenant with you" (6:17-18). Then comes the ultimate descriptor for Noah and for any who seek to serve God in their generation: "Noah did everything exactly as God commanded him" (6:22).

When the time came to board the ark, God reminded Noah of why he had been given this epochal task. "Go into the ark with your whole household, because among this generation I've seen that you are a moral man" (Genesis 7:1). I think it is proper to say that God judges each of us within the definitions of our generation. I am impatient with twenty-first-century pundits who pass judgment on how our ancestors handled their social and economic problems in other centuries, from Plymouth Rock to the vast frontier. Their opinions are akin to the eight-year-old who, when hearing the story of Jacob leaving home for the long journey to the house of his Uncle Laban, wonders why Jacob didn't text his mother along the way. Our assignment is to be as right as possible in our generation and to pray that we will leave something of worth for generations to come.

A New Testament writer calls Noah "a preacher of righteousness" (2 Peter 2:5), but he was one who had to be satisfied with winning over his own household. Considering the mindset to which he was preaching, Noah did very well. After all, the general thinking of his time had room only for thoughts of evil. As the ark was closed, eight persons were aboard: Noah, his wife, his sons (Shem, Ham, and Japheth) and their respective wives, along with "two of every creature that breathes" (Genesis 7:15). We're told that Noah (true to his character) did "just as God had commanded him" (7:16).

The Confusions in the Story

The Flood story seems to have discrepancies. For instance, God instructs Noah to take on the ark "a pair, male and female," of every living creature (Genesis 6:19-20); then a few verses later we read, "From every clean animal, take seven pairs, a male and his mate" (7:2); then in Genesis 7:8-9 we read, "From the clean and unclean animals, from the birds and everything crawling on the ground, two of each, male and female, went into the ark with Noah, just as God commanded Noah." Most contemporary biblical scholars feel that Genesis is the work of several ancient writers, brought together by a later compiler. Thus the inspired compiler becomes the significant author.

But Isaac Bashevis Singer, the great twentieth-century novelist, argues with the scholars. "Yet I am sure it was the same master writer, who knew exactly where his pen was leading him. . . . There is perfection in these stories, written by a single genius, from whom all writers can and should learn."[2]

In any event, don't miss the truth of the story.

The story is marked by several symbols. When the ark was ready to go, "the LORD closed the door behind them" (Genesis 7:16). This was the mark of divine finality. Those within were utterly secure; no person and no power could take their safety from them. For those outside, the last chance of entry was gone. The rain continued for forty days and nights (Forty is a biblical symbol of judgment or testing.). Both factors were at work here: The rain was judgment on the sins of the world; and it was a time of testing for those on the ark because after continuous days of rain, they surely must have wondered if it would ever end. Also, the flood of water was a symbol of cleansing, and thus—as the New Testament writer saw it—a symbol of baptism (1 Peter 3:20-22). It is, however, a mixed and in some ways a confusing symbol in that the flood waters "cleansed" the earth in judgment, while the family of Noah was untouched by the water

The Flood itself has a particular dramatic quality. We are told in the Creation story that "the LORD God hadn't yet sent rain on the earth, . . . though a stream rose from the earth and watered all of the fertile land" (Genesis 2:5-6). When the Flood came, there was an engulfing of water from above and below: "On that day all the springs of the deep sea erupted, and the windows in the skies opened" (7:11). It was as if the forces of nature combined to show their distress with the evil that had been done by humanity's sins: the visible sins of conduct, the heard sins of speech, and the corrupt thoughts of the mind where all conduct begins. There was no escaping the judgment. Look up or look down, the water was coming from both directions. Judgment surrounded on all sides.

A God of Judgment?

What shall we say of this disaster, of lives destroyed en masse, of nature in violent eruption? First, the Bible portrays a world that is so structured for righteousness that it revolts against sin. There is moral beauty in this fact; but we understand it only if we comprehend the unthinkable horror of sin, that sin is ultimately incompatible with God's world.

Second, sin always has consequences. Some sins are related to our conduct, with unhappy results for the sinner, for other persons, and for nonhuman creatures. But probably more consequences are built into the orderliness of our universe than we yet realize. One thing is sure. Since we humans have been designated overseers of this planet, a great deal of what is right about it and what is wrong with it seems to rest upon us. At the least we should do no more harm, and we should try to correct whatever we see that is out of harmony with God's plan.

Third, God is grieved by human sinfulness. The extent of the pain that comes with sin suggests the degree of divine pain. The point of the suffering is always redemption. It is not a matter of God getting a pound of flesh but of the restoration of the person, the institution, or the nation.

Fourth, the judgment is itself an evidence of God's love for humanity and for all creation. God doesn't give up on us.

Genesis tells us, "God remembered Noah" and all that was on the ark; and "God sent a wind over the earth so that the waters receded. The springs of the deep sea and the skies closed up" (8:1-2). God employed nature, once an agent of judgment, to cause the waters to recede and the healing of the earth to begin.

Are Natural Disasters God's Judgment?

The speed and global reach of contemporary news coverage brings reports of natural disasters right into our homes, workplaces, and smart phones almost every week. The images of widespread devastation from earthquakes, tsunamis, hurricanes, tornadoes, blizzards, and the like disturb us. The scale of disaster is often so great that everything seems in jeopardy, reminiscent of the great flood in Genesis 6–9. We sometimes wonder, Is all this death and destruction God's judgment on the sins of the stricken communities? What do we make of it all?

At a *scientific* level, we can account for earthquakes and tsunamis in terms of shifting tectonic plates, which make it possible for resources to well up from the deep, replenishing the surface of the earth. At a scientific level, we recognize that the atmospheric circulation of heat and moisture so necessary for life on our planet can also wreak havoc in tornadoes and hurricanes.

But how should we understand natural disasters at a *faith* level? What wisdom can we garner from the Bible, in particular, from the story of the Flood in Genesis?

It is important to note that even *after* the Flood, God recognized that human beings universally and inevitably have a bent toward sinning. "The ideas of the human mind," God realizes, "are evil from their youth" (Genesis 8:21). Yet even so, God refuses to reject or abandon or destroy humankind.

Note, too, that the dependable cycles of nature, first established by God at Creation (Genesis 1:14), then set aside for the Flood, have been restored by God (8:22). Judgment has been replaced by providential care evident in the natural world for "as long as the earth exists."

Further, Genesis 9:8-17 testifies to God's solemn promise—signified by the rainbow—never again to use world destruction as an act of punishment. This new covenant embraces all life on earth, human and nonhuman. Just as God originally brought creation out of chaos, God now pledges not to allow chaos to reclaim the world.

We know from the rest of the biblical story that human sin will repeatedly deserve and receive divine punishment. But natural disasters are not properly seen as the instruments of that punishment. We have it on good authority that the Creator who is also our heavenly Father "makes the sun rise on both the evil and the good and sends rain on both the righteous and the unrighteous" (Matthew 5:45).

Noah's first recorded act as he left the ark was to build "an altar to the LORD" (Genesis 8:20). This is the first reference to an altar since the Cain and Abel story. God was pleased and vowed never again to curse the earth "because of human beings since the ideas of the human mind are evil from their youth" (8:21) and gave Noah the sign of this covenant with the "bow in the clouds" (9:13). It is a covenant between God "and all creatures on earth" (9:17). We humans, however, are the only earth inhabitants who can complicate the covenant by how we use nature.

Noah was such an altogether heroic figure that we feel all must now have been well. But we humans are, well, human. Noah "made a new start and planted a vineyard" (Genesis 9:20). He drank the wine and became drunk, then lay naked in his tent. Ham was the first to discover his father's nakedness. When he told his brothers, they brought a robe to cover their father and approached him backward so they wouldn't see his nakedness. Ham's punishment for his act of disrespect was the curse uttered against his son Canaan.

So many questions and insights clamor for attention in this story. Let me mention just a few. For one, Noah demonstrates that even the best of us humans can err, and err badly. The Bible makes no effort to explain or excuse Noah's conduct, nor should we. But we never sin to ourselves alone; always someone else is hurt. In this case it was Noah's son Ham and Noah's grandson Canaan. Mind you, Ham's deed was his own; and he was cursed for it. But the door to his sin was opened by his father. When, like Ham, we discover the nakedness—the failures—of our progenitors (whether within our personal story or as historians or social critics), we should deal with these failures with the kind of gracious integrity that we hope future generations will give us.

Live the Story

No matter how dark the human scene, God is still at work in our world. Sometimes God's work is judgment—not because God is vengeful, but because God is redemptive. In every cloud of judgment there is the rainbow of grace. At what times and places in your life have you felt the pain (and perhaps embarrassment) of judgment? Did you eventually come to feel that something good had come from the experience? How so?

While we humans bring trouble on ourselves, we also are the means by which God saves the day, the institution, or the generation. In a time when "humanity had become thoroughly evil on the earth" (Genesis 6:5), "Noah was a moral and exemplary man" (6:9). Who among your contemporaries seems to be living an exemplary life, in sharp contrast to the prevailing culture? What stands in the way of you leading such an exemplary life?

Nevertheless, Noah himself was human. As he and his family stepped from the ark, they were reminded that they had been made "in the divine image" (Genesis 9:6) and that they were now to "populate the earth, and multiply in it" (9:7). It sounds like a repeat of Genesis 1 and 2, with a whole new beginning. But the beginning is still with us human beings, and Noah and his sons prove it.

The assignment for you and me? By God's grace, to do better. Spend a few minutes considering what that might entail in your daily life.

1 From A Tale of Two Cities, by Charles Dickens, in The Oxford Dictionary of Quotations, edited by Elizabeth Knowles (Oxford University Press, 2004); page 272.
2 From "Genesis," by Isaac Bashevis Singer, in Congregation: Contemporary Writers Read the Jewish Bible, edited by David Rosenberg (Harcourt Brace Jovanovich, 1987); page 7.

4.

Rebellion and Dispersal

Genesis 10:1–11:9

Claim Your Story

"After the flood, Noah lived 350 years" (Genesis 9:28). We're told nothing of what he did in those years, nor do we get further reflection on the moral quality that made him the singular voice of redemption during an era of moral corruption. The story moves instead to his sons. Here, too, nothing is said by way of either achievement or failure; only a listing of their descendants is provided.

The old question now comes anew: What will humanity do with its new start? We are told that Noah soiled his story somewhat, and his son Ham as well, as if to remind us that humans after the Flood will be as erratic as before. But those are individual stories. Will there be any action that seems to speak for the larger body of the human race?

We don't have to wait long. In a valley in the land of Shinar, humanity organizes against what seems to be the plan of God; and they set out to build a tower that will be the rallying place for their rebellion. God frustrates these efforts, confuses their language, and thus disperses the people.

What is the meaning of this story of the tower of Babel? Does it say anything about cities? Is God opposed to the unity of the human race? What is the writer of Genesis telling us about the meaning and purpose of language and the gift of communication? And what does any of this mean to life as you and I know it today?

Enter the Bible Story

Genesis 10 is a kind of reprise of Genesis 5—names, names, names, with little else to offer a plot. But as we read carefully, we pick up some fascinating details. A careful scholar notes that there are seventy names in the table of nations in this chapter. Numbers are used significantly throughout the Bible, and especially in the Hebrew Scriptures. Seven is the number of completeness; thus seventy, a major multiple of seven, suggests that this is the whole body, so to speak, of nations, a kind of complete atlas in a few lines.

Most of the names are novel to us and without meaning. But several stand out: Egypt, Assyria, Babylon, and Canaan. These names will recur in Israel's history and thus from a theological point of view will become elements in the salvation story. We might see them largely as negatives, but this is not a complete evaluation. Each of these nations also has its positive role to play at some point in the grand story.

Enter Nimrod, the Mighty

You will remember that the stylized biographies in Genesis 5 were interrupted by a notable exception, Enoch, the man who "walked with God." So, too, there is an exception in Genesis 10: Nimrod. The CEB translation describes him as "the first great warrior on earth," with the additional line, "and so it is said, 'Like Nimrod, whom the LORD saw as a great hunter.' " (Genesis 10:8-9). Professor Alter's translation says, "He was the first mighty man on the earth."[1] I think Professor Leon Kass gets to the heart of the matter when he reminds us that Nimrod's name means "rebelliousness" and translates Nimrod's descriptive phrase, "a powerful hunter in the face of God."[2]

Some things are clear. Nimrod was more than a bow and arrow hunter, more than an ancient provider with a touch of the modern sportsman. We get an idea of Nimrod's might and of his "warrior" abilities when we read, "The most important cities in his kingdom were Babel, Erech, Accad and Calneh in the land of Shinar" (Genesis 10:10). (Whether there is also significance in Nimrod being the grandson of Ham, Noah's disgraced son, I will leave to a novelist to explore. But it's an interesting psycho-logical byroad.)

Without a doubt Nimrod is the key figure in this chapter and in the drama that follows in the Babel story. Consider that one of "the important cities" in Nimrod's domain was Babel and that all of his empire was in the land of Shinar, where the crisis of the tower of Babel occurred. Consider, too, the quality of character that is inferred in the meaning of Nimrod's name. And consider especially the idea that he was a "hunter in the face of God." We need to have all of this in mind as we try to understand what happens in Genesis 11 and why it is that God's judgment fell so decisively on what appears on the surface simply to have been an ambitious archi-tectural project, the first skyscraper.

Language, the Human Glory

Language is the wonder of us human creatures, the seismic difference between us and the rest of earth's inhabitants. Students of bird life have determined that some birds have a "vocabulary" of perhaps two dozen calls, having to do mostly with warnings of danger or locations of food or mating calls. We can teach a horse or dog the meaning of certain com-mand words but not how to carry on a verbal conversation. With great effort researchers have developed simian vocabularies with several dozen words. But today, Marilyn Chandler McEntyre reminds us, "the English language has over a million words. The average educated person knows about 20,000 words and uses about 2,000 in a week."[3]

I would dare submit that words are the greatest power entrusted to us humans. All the other powers—political, educational, economic, social—depend on words for their exercise. But with power comes peril. Words can convey love ("How do I love thee? / Let me count the ways."[4]), or comfort ("The LORD is my shepherd, I shall not want" [Psalm 23:1, NRSV].), or the struggle of decision ("To be, or not to be: that is the ques-tion."[5]). But words can also be the conveyor of hatred or deception or pornography. Words are the instrument of the Gospel of John and of Adolf Hitler, the redemptive words of a true pastor or the cheap fraud of the charlatan. No gift entrusted to human beings carries anything like the potential of words for salvation or for damnation.

So when Genesis says, "All people on the earth had one language and the same words" (11:1), it is telling us not only that the potential for community and communication was great but also that many other possibilities lay open for the human race. In Eden, God had talked with Adam and Eve; but so had the serpent. Now humans had settled in a valley in Shinar and said, "Come, let's make bricks and bake them hard" (11:3). That is, they had learned by their building skills that some products lasted better than others; and they intended that this building would be one that would last.

They had a particular goal in mind. "Come, let's build for ourselves a city and a tower with its top in the sky, and let's make a name for ourselves so that we won't be dispersed over all the earth" (Genesis 11:4). A fascinating kind of isolationism was at work. They had no way of knowing if there were other humans in other places, and they didn't want to know. They saw themselves as the earth's only occupants. They had no idea what lay beyond the farther reach of hills, and they didn't care to find out. Perhaps they were haunted by the memory of a tradition, that their human assignment was to "fill the earth and master it" (1:28), and they really didn't care to get involved with all of the earth. Or, on the other hand, perhaps they had a mythic memory of an Eden from which their ancestors had been expelled, and they didn't intend to suffer that kind of fate again. Perhaps the valley in Shinar seemed to be the closest to Eden they might ever get. In any event, they intended to resist dispersion and to build "a tower with its top in the sky" (11:4).

To construct such a tower, the people would need precision in planning and communication. God said, "Come, let's go down and mix up their language there so they won't understand each other's language" (Genesis 11:7). No doubt this story is intended to suggest the birth of different languages, but I think it means more than that. I believe it also describes the breakdown of communication that goes further than language, important as language is.

We describe this idea in a phrase that sometimes arises in discussions. When we find ourselves in deep agreement with another person, we say, with satisfaction, "Now we're talking the same language!" By contrast, when failure of communication becomes very frustrating, someone says, "It's easy to see that we're not even talking the same language." This has nothing to do with words as such but with our ability or our willingness to understand the other person, that is, to find a place where we can grasp one another's point of view. It's possible that even then we will still disagree, but at least we will know where the differences lie. That clarity regarding our misunderstanding is itself a key kind of understanding.

At this point in our story, the people ceased to understand each other; and the Lord "dispersed them from there over all of the earth, and they stopped building the city" (Genesis 11:8).

What's So Bad About the City?

William Cowper, the eighteenth-century poet, wrote, "God made the country, and man made the town."[6] A century earlier, another English

Across the Testaments

The Country and the City

The ideal of the Hebrew Scriptures is the garden of Eden; by contrast the city seems personified in the spirit of Cain and the arrogance of Nimrod. One would expect the New Testament to celebrate the same theme, and in a measure it does. Our Lord was crucified in Jerusalem, the major city in Judaism; and the writer of Revelation picks up the Babel/Babylon theme in his description of the conflict between good and evil: "Babylon the great, the mother of prostitutes and the vile things of the earth" (17:5). The beginning of the end of evil is symbolized with the fall of this iconic city: "Babylon, you great city, you powerful city! In a single hour your judgment has come" (18:10).

But when John sees the new heaven and the new earth, it is not a garden but a *city*, "the holy city, Jerusalem, coming down out of heaven from God" (Revelation 21:10). It is splendid in its beauty and redemptive by nature; its river is "life-giving water" (22:1), and "the tree's leaves are for the healing of the nations" (22:2). It is as if the city is the new Eden.

poet and essayist, Abraham Cowley, made the same point with biblical allusions: "God the first garden made, and the first city Cain."[7] Surely it seems significant that the first recorded instance of a city is the one the murderer, Cain, made for his son and named for him. Is there something inherently bad in the city?

As someone who fell in love with New York City when I lived there briefly as a young man and on the basis of the great Samuel Johnson's words about another great city, "When a man is tired of London, he is tired of life,"[8] I'm compelled to be careful what I say about the city. But it can be said that a city seems to make individuals less valuable. There is irony in the way the multitudes of people in a city incline the city dweller to be lonely and the individual to be overlooked. Geographers tell us that our world is becoming increasingly urban; in large areas one drives simply from one city to another without seeing any true countryside. I ponder, on the other hand, the current sociological movement to rebuild our cities so that they become a compilation of neighborhoods that are essentially small towns, each complete in itself, largely accessible on foot.

Professor Kass insists that "Babel is not just any city but is *the* city, the paradigmatic or universal city, representing a certain universal human aspiration."[9] Thus Babel was not necessarily condemned for its size or its close-bounded style of living but for the attitude that impelled it. It was a congregant body united in rebellion against God, led by a man named "Rebellion," Nimrod. It seems to me that there is something peculiarly intoxicating about a great city, the feeling that one can conquer the world. But perhaps I say that only because I was a young man when I lived in New York City or perhaps because for generations the young have wanted to "move to the city," the place where they expect to fulfill their dreams.

The story of Babel—or Babylon, to use the name that makes this city symbolic all the way to the Book of Revelation—is the first full-scale story of humanity challenging God. Adam and Eve disobeyed God, but with a kind of stupid innocence, hardly realizing what they were doing. Cain built a city and named it for his son, a deed for which in a sense I praise him: He was thinking not simply of his own place in history (a place already marked by shame), but of a place of meaning for his son. But "Let's make a name for *ourselves*" was the mood of Babel.

The bricks of Babel are also significant. The plains of Shinar didn't offer the natural building materials to be found in the mountains, so the people made bricks ("brick bricks" is the literal Hebrew). "Come, let's make bricks and bake them hard" (Genesis 11:3). A new order of proud craftsmen was at work, developing new technologies, the computers of that day. This is the first biblical reference to bricks. We will not read of them again until Exodus, when they became a particularly significant part of the suffering of Israelite slavery (Exodus 1:14).

Note also the tower, "with its top in the sky" (Genesis 11:4). The tower may have been a plan for safety, in the context of the Flood, as Professor Kass notes, "an artificial high ground providing refuge against future floods and a watchtower for the plain; it is even imaginable that it might be intended as a pillar to hold up heaven, lest it crack open another time."[10] And particularly, it seems to me, the aim of making its "top in the sky" was a declaration that with the tower this city would eventually dismiss God from the throne.

Is this kind of arrogance endemic to the city? I don't think so. We humans have a capacity, it seems, for challenging God, whether in desert or garden, field or city. But by its very magnificence, its architecture, its centers for culture and entertainment, the city is a breeding place for

About the Christian Faith

The Sacred and the Secular

The issue in the tower of Babel could well be summarized as the conflict of the sacred and the secular, with Babylon being the ultimate "secular city," to use a term popular in mid-twentieth-century theology. At its best, Christianity has sought to redeem the secular. In a sense, this is the essence of the Incarnation: The Word became flesh, to dwell among us, "full of grace and truth" (John 1:14). But, of course, the secular asserts itself, seeking always to build its tower; and the relationship of the sacred and the secular is always in controversy.

human arrogance. It is not reminded daily, as is the farm, that its future depends on nature and the God of nature. Only at times of dramatic climatic action do city dwellers realize their helplessness. It's hard to be humble when you're so big. Even when that bigness demonstrates that you may not be able to govern yourself, you find a kind of perverse glory in the problem.

In any event, the story is about to go on. Cities will continue, until in our day they will be more dominant and demanding than ever. But just now the languages are confused, and the population is being "dispersed over all the earth" (Genesis 11:4).

Live the Story

You and I live in an urbanized world. Wherever we live, the urban culture asserts itself. Thus whether we love the city or are frustrated by it, we must learn how to live with it. As people of faith, we must do still more: We must become redemptive residents of our valley of Shinar. We will also want to know how to relate to the towers that are built in our time. Every day offers new headlines of new discoveries, new research, new and unbelievable achievements. Some are little more than an invitation to spend our money to gain the latest thing. Others challenge our very purpose in living. All lay some claim to the most important of our human resources: *time*. Nimrod's generation invested itself in just one tower of human aspiration. Our generation sees a new tower in full splendor before the previous one is fully occupied.

As for communication, these are strange times. The English language has become so pervasive that it might almost be said that we live in a pre-Babel world. Marilyn McEntyre reminds us, "More than half of the world's technical and scientific periodicals and three-quarters of the world's mail are in English. About 80 percent of the information stored in the world's computers is in English. English is transmitted to more than 100 million people a day by the five largest broadcasting companies."[11] Nevertheless, it is clear that we're not communicating. In times of political decision-making, we discover that a minority are talking with one another; rather, we talk at the other. And whether the talk radio stations specialize in sports or politics, most seem to seek confirmation rather than information.

Can the believer season such a culture with a humility to listen, to moderate, and to empathize to a point where our society will hear better? The challenge is great.

1 From *The Five Books of Moses*, by Robert Alter (W.W. Norton, 2004); page 55.

2 From *The Beginning of Wisdom*, by Leon R. Kass (The University of Chicago Press, 2003); page 222.

3 From *Caring for Words in a Culture of Lies*, by Marilyn Chandler McEntyre (William B. Eerdmans, 2009); page 8.

4 From *Sonnets From the Portuguese*, Number 43, by Elizabeth Barrett Browning, in *The Oxford Dictionary of Quotations*, edited by Elizabeth Knowles (Oxford University Press, 2004); page 158.

5 From *Hamlet*, by William Shakespeare; Act 3, Scene 1, Line 56, in *The Oxford Dictionary of Quotations*; page 686.

6 From *The Task*, by William Cowper; Bk. 1, "The Sofa," Line 749, in *The Oxford Dictionary of Quotations*; page 247.

7 From "The Garden," by Abraham Cowley, in *Essays, in Verse and Prose*, in *The Oxford Dictionary of Quotation*; page 245.

8 From *Life of Samuel Johnson*, by James Boswell; see http://www.samueljohnson.com/tiredlon.html. (3-15-11)

9 From *The Beginning of Wisdom*, by Leon R. Kass; page 223.

10 From *The Beginning of Wisdom*, by Leon R. Kass; page 229.

11 From *Caring for Words in a Culture of Lies*, by Marilyn Chandler McEntyre; page 8.

5.

Abraham and the Turn of History

Genesis 11:10–23:20

Claim Your Story

On the surface our generation seems to have a contradiction. American colleges and universities currently offer few courses in history because of diminishing interest in the subject; yet there's a growing interest in biographies, and the pursuit of personal genealogies has become a major hobby. Let me put it another way. Ask your friends at a social gathering to name the greatest influence in their lives. Someone may name a particular war, or perhaps a particular social movement or a highly publicized public event. But a majority will name a person—a parent, a teacher, a coach, a tutor, a Big Brother or Big Sister, a clergyperson, a friend. Who is it that comes to your mind as a major influence in your life?

Perhaps history versus biography is not really a contradiction at all. Ralph Waldo Emerson clarified the matter for us: "There is properly no history; only biography."[1] True, our human history is made up of war, politics, famines, movements, and inventions; but all of these start with or center around *persons*.

In this study you are about to meet a very important figure of history, one who has influenced your life and mine. Three of the world's major religions (Judaism, Christianity, and Islam) claim their origin in him. His name is Abraham (or Abram, when he is first introduced to us). Many Jewish and Christian scholars say that the opening chapters of Genesis serve primarily to set the stage for his entrance into the biblical story.

I offer him as a turning point in human history. If that be so, it's time we studied his biography, not only to get a better understanding of our history, but to see more clearly who you and I are. Who was this man, and how did God use him? What does he mean to us today? And what is his role in our salvation story?

Enter the Bible Story

Abraham enters the biblical story in a kind of crowd scene. If it were a movie, it would at first be hard to pick Abraham out of the crowd—and after the camera finds him, we might wonder for a time why it lingers on this particular figure. The "crowd scene" in Genesis 11 is a list of the descendants of Shem, a series of forgettable persons who had a son and then "had other sons and daughters" (11:11, for example).

No other details enter the routine until the writer introduces us to Terah, who "became the father of Abram, Nahor, and Haran" (Genesis 11:26). We're told that Haran died while the family was still in their native land, in Ur of the Chaldeans, which was a major city of the ancient world. We're given another detail, that Abram and Nahor married; and still more, we learn the names of their wives. This is the first identification of women by name since Eve, except for the somewhat sidewise reference to three women in the lives of Lamech and Tubal-cain (Genesis 4:22-23).

We know the plot is thickening, however, when Genesis notes that Sarai, Abram's wife, "was barren; she had no child" (11:30, NRSV). The repetitive statement suggests the hopelessness of her situation and probably also makes clear that she and Abram had not resorted to arranging for a child to be born through a maid, which was a common practice at the time for continuing a family line when a wife was unable to conceive. The writer is setting us up for a divine miracle by making clear that we have a complicated situation here. We learn further that this extended family left Ur and got as far as the town of Haran and "settled there" until Terah died (Genesis 11:31-32).

God Called Abram

The Bible's salvation story has preludes in the story of Adam and Eve's fall and in the ministry of Noah. But now the salvation story has a clear focus. (By "salvation story" I mean the record of God's effort to save our human race from the specter of sin and death, as introduced to us in the story of Adam and Eve's sin in Eden.) The focus is on the family of Abraham. The focus will continue there through the Hebrew Scriptures and the New Testament, even to the Book of Revelation.

God's call to Abram was direct and insistent. In one of his most moving poems, the Benedictine monk Kilian McDonnell refers to this call as "imperious," with "no letter of introduction."[2] In truth, it was not so much a call as a command. "The LORD said to Abram, 'Leave your land, your family, and your father's household for the land that I will show you.' " (Genesis 12:1). But a promise came with the command: "I will make of you a great nation and will bless you. I will make your name respected, and you will be a blessing" (12:2). Then the promise took on universal significance:

> I will bless those who bless you,
>   those who curse you I will curse;
>   all the families of earth
>   will be blessed because of you.
> (Genesis 12:3)

At this point we know that the course of salvation history has been set, that it includes "all the families of earth" and will work its way out through a particular nation-family. People of faith—people like you and me—need to know that God's plan has ancient roots and an eternal destiny. It is important to know this because from the beginning the plan has unfolded in what often have been hostile circumstances so that sometimes even the most resolute believers may wonder what the end of the story will be. You and I need to know that God is still at work in our generation, redeeming "all the families of earth." This knowledge should inspire us to cooperate with God's call.

We learn quickly that God's call to Abram was against the odds. We already know that Sarai was barren; so when Abram was told that he would become "a great nation" (Genesis 12:2), we know the circumstances

Across the Testaments

Abram and Sarai the Heroic

When the writer of the New Testament Book of Hebrews gives us the honor roll of faith heroes, more space is given to Abraham and Sarah than to Abel, Enoch, Noah, Isaac, Jacob, and Joseph combined. Abraham and Sarah are made symbolic of all those persons who "died in faith without receiving the promises," people who "make it clear that they are looking for a homeland" because "they are longing for a better country, that is, a heavenly one" (Hebrews 11:13, 14, 16). Thus Abraham becomes a Kingdom person, one of those who dare to pray, "Thy kingdom come. Thy will be done in earth, as it is in heaven" (Matthew 6:10, KJV) and who seek to live and work accordingly. Only rarely in the Old Testament are there hints of a belief in eternal life; but the writer of Hebrews sees Abraham and Sarah and other faith figures as persons who have caught a glimpse of "a better country, that is, a heavenly one."

were negative. Now we learn that "Abram was 75 years old" (12:4). Later we will learn that Sarai was just 10 years younger. That is, Abram and Sarai didn't hold much promise as progenitors of "a great nation."

Nevertheless, like Noah, Abram did "just as the LORD told him" (Genesis 12:4). He gathered together all his possessions and left Haran. We don't know how many were in Abram's employ at this time, but later we learn that he had over three hundred men of military age; so we can see that when Abram left Haran, he was putting a substantial corporate headquarters on hoof and wheel.

Abram's first recorded stop was at "the sacred place at Shechem, at the oak of Moreh" (Genesis 12:6). Here Abram built an altar to the Lord. Then he moved on to a place between Bethel and Ai and again built an altar. Abram's journey would be marked by his altar-building. Every biography is written around some kind of landmark. For a business executive, it is corporate acquisitions; for the political leader, it is elections; for the athlete, it is records set or broken; for many, it is the places where they've lived or where their children were born. For Abram, it was altars. The altars marked his spiritual journey, his growing relationship with God. And it is Abram's spiritual journey—not his remarkable executive skills or demonstration of military intelligence, but his walk with God—that makes him stand out.

Abram's Uneven Journey

The Bible is a forthright, honest book. It portrays its saints with warts and all. Notable as Abraham was (In the Book of Isaiah he is referred to as God's "friend" [41:8, NRSV].), the course of his life and of the divine friendship was uneven. He was a man of great faith, but that faith seems to have faltered when he and Sarai made a trip into Egypt. Abram explained to Sarai that because she was an attractive woman, he was afraid the Egyptians might kill him in order to have her. He said, "So tell them you are my sister so that they will treat me well for your sake, and I will survive because of you" (Genesis 12:13).

The deception worked. "Things went well for Abram because of her: he acquired flocks, cattle, male donkeys, men servants, women servants, female donkeys, and camels" (Genesis 12:16). But when God struck Pharaoh's house with a plague, Pharaoh realized he had been deceived and ordered Abram to leave. Nevertheless, he left with great gains. We wonder how Abram could so abuse his wife, Sarai, and how it was that though he had faith enough to leave Haran and follow God into the unknown, his faith wasn't enough to make him secure when he got to Egypt. And we wonder still more how he could attempt the same deception years later in Gerar (Genesis 20).

But Abram's character and faith shone when his fortunes and the fortunes of his nephew, Lot, became too great for an area to support them both. Abram—though the elder and in a sense the guardian of Lot—gave Lot first choice of the land and gladly took what was left (Genesis 13). Abram was generous again when with the men of his household he rescued not only Lot, but a consortium of five kings after they had been taken captive in battle, and then refused the usual plunder of war (Genesis 14).

At this point God reassured Abram: "I am your protector. Your reward will be very great" (Genesis 15:1). Now Abram confessed his doubt. Since he still had no children, would Eliezer, the head of his household, be his only heir? This expression of fear had been long in coming. I sense that the prosperity that had come Abram's way had only increased his wonder that God had not blessed Sarai and him with a child.

We know nothing about the conversations between Abram and Sarai through these years, but at last Sarai made a vigorous suggestion: "The LORD has kept me from giving birth, so go to my servant [Hagar]. Maybe she will provide me with children" (Genesis 16:2). Abram agreed, and Hager conceived. But the "success"—a success that came because Abram and Sarai had compromised God's original promise—carried a huge price. Jealousy and enmity came between Sarai and her maid. Hagar was cast from the household. God restored Hagar, however; and she and her son, Ishmael, made their home there until the birth of Isaac fourteen years later, when they were permanently expelled. Arabic peoples traditionally claim Ishmael as the father of their ethnic group.

Isaac Was Born

God continued to reassure Abram at intervals. In time God established a physical symbol of the covenant that existed with Abram, the mark of circumcision. With it came a promise: "You will be the ancestor of many nations" (Genesis 17:4). At this same time, God announced that Abram's name would now be Abraham, "ancestor of a multitude" (17:5, translators' footnote c), and that Sarai's name would become Sarah

About the Scripture
Regarding Hagar's Child

Sarai's first recorded speech is her appeal to Abram to solve the problem of their barrenness by taking her servant Hagar as his wife, with the understanding that if Hagar conceived, the child would be Sarai's. Professor Robert Alter writes, "The institution of surrogate maternity to which she [Sarai] resorts is by no means her invention, being well attested in ancient Near Eastern legal documents."[3] It is interesting to compare this ancient solution to childlessness with some of our contemporary practices. The biblical story artfully demonstrates that while some things can be worked out legally, human issues may nevertheless arise. In the Sarai-Hagar story, a bitter rivalry developed between the two women.

(17:15). But "Abraham fell on his face and laughed" at the thought of a child being born to such aged parents (17:17). He then said to God, "If only you would accept Ishmael!" (17:18). Isaac was to be the child of promise, however, the child of faith; and at last he was born and was named, appropriately, "he laughs" (17:19, translators' footnote d), perhaps because Abraham had laughed at the prospect of having a child with Sarah and Sarah, too, had laughed at the thought. Or perhaps Isaac's name suggests that the last laugh was God's.

In the year before Isaac's birth, Abraham's relationship with God got a still greater dimension. When it was revealed to Abraham that the cities of Sodom and Gomorrah would be destroyed for the seriousness of their sins, Abraham pleaded for their preservation (Genesis 18:16-33). The scene is one of the most remarkable in all of biblical literature, much like Moses' appeal for his people generations later (Exodus 32:30-32). The dialogue between Abraham and God was both majestic and humorous. Abraham bargained like a shopper in a Middle Eastern bazaar; and God heard him patiently, never ceasing to grant his requests until Abraham ceased asking. But even when Abraham had brought the possible quota of righteous souls in Sodom and Gomorrah down to ten, the standard was too high. In terms of the quality of evil, these cities were like the culture of

About the Christian Faith

The Nature of God

From Genesis onward the Scriptures portray God as *person*. God is more than a principle or an impersonal force; rather, God is One who communicates with humanity and finds pleasure in humanity's response. This concept is shown in God's communication in the garden of Eden and in God's partnership with Noah but especially in God's relationship with Abraham and Sarah. Abraham dared to reason with God about Sodom and Gomorrah, and God was pleased to respond to Abraham's efforts. Abraham and Sarah laughed at the promise of a child; but God was patient, not offended. When Jesus said that with God, the very hairs of our head are counted (Matthew 10:30), careful readers of the Hebrew Scriptures are ready to understand this picture of God's character. It is consistent with our understanding of the nature of God.

Noah's time. Eventually, only Lot and his two daughters were saved. But Abraham had pleaded the cause with the passion of a true intercessor.

Isaac is portrayed as a miracle, but he was much more than that. He was the living symbol of the covenant between God and Abraham. God had called Abraham to be the father of "a great nation" (Genesis 12:2) and said to him, "All the families of earth will be blessed because of you" (12:3). Thus the call that came to Abraham in the iconic story in Genesis 22 was even more than the poignant human drama in which it was set. The thought of a father going with his child to a place of sacrifice, knowing that the child is to be the sacrifice, tests our sensibilities to the limit—as it is meant to do. The monstrous horror of the story is intended to convey to us both the greatness of the faith issue and the consummate trust that is portrayed in the friendship of God and Abraham.

The character of both was at stake. If Abraham had refused to act, his refusal would have violated his covenant with God. If God had allowed the sacrifice of Isaac, it would have violated all that Scripture subsequently tells us about the nature of God.

It is clear that Abraham felt that God would somehow intervene. As he and Isaac began the climax of their journey to the mount of sacrifice, Abraham told his servants to wait where they were. "The boy and I will walk up there, worship, and then come back to you" (Genesis 22:5). That is, Abraham was telling his servants that he and Isaac would return. In the brief detail that follows, the writer uses the same stark sentence twice: "The two of them walked on together" (22:6, 8). The only recorded dialogue is when the boy asks, "Where is the lamb for the entirely burned offering?" and the father answers, "God will see to it, my son" (22:7-8). See, too, the pathos. In these brief exchanges Abraham addressed Isaac not by his name, but by their relationship: "my son."

Live the Story

What does Abraham's story mean to you and me? At a religious level, it reminds us, as we noted earlier, that the three monotheistic faiths (Judaism, Christianity, and Islam) all claim their origin in Abraham. From a political point of view, we ponder that the ongoing conflict in the Middle East seems still to be the Ishmael-Isaac conflict. One sees it in the news media nearly every day, and the religious leaders on both sides lay claim to their heritage in Abraham.

From the point of view of vital, personal faith, we watch Abraham with awe. We recognize that—like all of us—he was at times a flawed human being who sometimes demonstrated his faith by his lapses. But we see also why he was called a "friend of God." He dared to follow God against all odds, to challenge God on behalf of the condemned cities of Sodom and Gomorrah (partly for his nephew Lot's sake, of course, but I think also out of his affection for a populace he had previously delivered from their military captors). Then he demonstrated his ultimate trust on the lonely walk to Moriah. No wonder the New Testament uses Abraham as the exemplar of faith (Galatians and Hebrews) and of works (James). You and I can learn both faith and works as we immerse ourselves in the stories of Abraham and Sarah.

1 From *Essays* (1841), by Ralph Waldo Emerson, in *The Oxford Dictionary of Quotations*, edited by Elizabeth Knowles (Oxford University Press, 2004); page 307.
2 From "The Call of Abraham," by Kilian McDonnell, in *Swift, Lord, You Are Not* (Saint John's University Press, 2003); page 10.
3 From *The Five Books of Moses*, by Robert Alter (W.W. Norton, 2004); page 77.

6.

Isaac: A Sacred Interlude

Genesis 24:1–28:9

Claim Your Story

You and I don't get to choose the times into which we're born. You probably had some grade school teachers who told you to dream big because almost anything was possible if you set your mind to it. And some teacher or preacher or motivational speaker told you this was the greatest time in history to be alive. It's a good attitude to have toward life.

But perhaps you feel more kinship with Miniver Cheevy, the character described by the poet Edwin Arlington Robinson. "He wept that he was ever born"[1] because he wished for days long past, when warriors wore iron clothing instead of khaki suits and life had more glamour and romance.

I think of Miniver Cheevy when I read the biblical story of Isaac. And when I think of Isaac's story, I think of a great number of people I've known. A cynic might say that the high point of Isaac's life was when he was born and that it was all downhill after that. No child was ever wanted more than Isaac, but his life unfolded in generally ordinary ways.

What do you do if your generation is not one holding "a rendezvous with destiny"? What if you grow up in an ordinary town, in ordinary times, and you find that you're living out your life in ordinary days? They tell us that everybody is important; but how can you feel important when most of your time is spent just staying alive, paying your bills, and being on time for work or church or dinner? Where's the nobility or grandeur in that?

Enter the Bible Story

If I were a composer commissioned to write a symphony about the biblical stories of Abraham, Isaac, and Jacob, I would discover that their stories fit well into the usual movements of a symphony. Normally, the first movement is moderately fast, which fits Abraham's story very well, with its uprooting, its nomadic life, and its faith struggles. A symphony's third movement has a "dancelike quality," which takes on a triumphant mood if the third movement is also the last. This is just right for Jacob. The second movement is traditionally the slowest—made to order for Isaac!

These three men are the patriarchs of the biblical story. Their names are recited together throughout the Scriptures with the rhythm of authority. But each has his own distinct personality and his own unique role in the unfolding drama. Abraham and Jacob are dramatic figures—very different, except that each one dominates the scene wherever he appears. Not so with Isaac. Sometimes you hardly know he is part of the story, let alone a lead character.

Isaac's Special Role

What does such a person say to you and me? Isaac seems more often to be acted upon than to be the actor. The family had a great feast the day he was weaned. During the festivities Isaac's older half-brother, Ishmael, was laughing (Genesis 21:9). This upset Isaac's mother, Sarah; and she insisted that Ishmael and his mother, Hagar, be cast out of the family. This demand distressed Abraham because of his love for Ishmael, but he agreed to it. The infant Isaac was a tool for his mother's purposes. Some years later, as we have already noted, he became the agent in his father's great test of faith, a test that had to have been fully as crucial for Isaac as for Abraham. But we speak of it as Abraham's test, essentially forgetting Isaac's part.

The same kind of scenario unfolds when it is time for Isaac to marry. We hear nothing of his desires; his father takes all the initiative. Concerned lest Isaac marry "from the Canaanite women among whom" they live (Genesis 24:3), Abraham instructs "the oldest servant of his household" (24:2)—obviously the most trusted, the one who must have seen the continuing work of God in Abraham's life—"Go to my land and my family and find a wife for my son Isaac there" (24:4). But by no means should the servant take Isaac to Abraham's homeland. God had promised that Canaan was to be the family home; there was no going back.

The unnamed servant was faithful to his task. He performed it with a remarkable second-hand faith. "LORD, God of my master Abraham, make something good happen for me today and be loyal to my master Abraham" (Genesis 24:12). He didn't presume to address God for himself, but he pleaded his case on the ground of Abraham's need and spiritual character. I understand; and I venture you do, too. When I was a pastor, I often prayed for my church and its people on the ground of their need rather than on the basis of my own appeal; and I know that others often prayed for me in the same way.

The woman to whom the servant was led was Rebekah, granddaughter of Nahor and Milcah, Abraham's brother and sister-in-law. It is at this point that we meet Laban, Rebekah's older brother, who will become a larger figure in the story a little later. The writer of Genesis introduces Laban tellingly. He reports that Laban noticed "the ring and the bracelets on his sister's arms" (Genesis 24:30), gifts presented to her by the stranger from Canaan. Laban apparently had an eye for opportunity.

The story of Isaac and Rebekah seems more a business story than a love story. Isaac had no say in the matter. Not only was he not consulted in his father's commissioning of the servant and not only was he not part of the exploratory trip, when the servant told his mission to Rebekah's mother and brother, they asked Rebekah, "Will you go with this man?" and she answered simply, "I will go" (Genesis 24:58). It was apparently assumed that Isaac would be pleased with the arrangements when she arrived. Rebekah's household was very businesslike. In time we will see that Rebekah exercised the same businesslike skills.

So Rebekah traveled to Canaan. One evening when Isaac was inspecting his pastureland, he saw a caravan on the horizon, the caravan that was bringing his bride; and Rebekah saw him. Whether it was love at first sight we don't know, but it was marriage at first sight. When the servant told Isaac "everything that had happened" (Genesis 24:66), the author tells us that "Isaac brought Rebekah into his mother Sarah's tent. He married Rebekah and loved her. So Isaac found comfort after his mother's death" (24:67). I suspect that a twenty-first-century marriage counselor would find several interesting details in this story, as would a psychologist. Come to think of it, I sense that the Genesis author was himself a pretty fair psychologist. He used his narrative style well. Isaac was forty years old at the time. He loved his mother, whose death and burial are reported in Genesis 23, and missed her. She was probably his emotional support more than his father. But now Isaac loved Rebekah and found comfort with her in the absence of his mother. Love has many faces, and it fulfills many needs in our respective lives. We may idealize some expressions of love over others, but we do well to receive love always with thoughtful regard.

The Birth of Twins

Rebekah's family had sent her to Canaan with a prayer that she would become "thousands of ten thousand," that her children would "possess their enemies' cities" (Genesis 24:60). The blessing was slow in coming, however. Rebekah was unable to have children. Abraham's servant had prayed for guidance when he was seeking a wife for Isaac. Now Isaac "prayed to the LORD for his wife," "the LORD was moved by his prayer," and "Rebekah became pregnant" (25:21).

The pregnancy was quite difficult, however, so difficult that Rebekah said, "If this is what it's like, why did it happen to me?" (Genesis 25:22). Like Abraham's servant and like Isaac, she went to the Lord. She learned that there were "two nations" in her womb (25:23), two different peoples. Further, she learned that "one people will be stronger than the other; / the older will serve the younger" (25:23). I'm sure Rebekah never forgot this. We don't know if Isaac ever knew. When the twins were born, the younger was "gripping" the heel of the older (25:26), as if already striving for mastery. The older was named Esau, for his physical appearance (He was "red all over, clothed with hair" [25:25]; and Esau meant "red."); and the younger was named Jacob, for his heel-grabbing. By this time Isaac was sixty years old. It had been a long wait, though short compared with Abraham and Sarah's wait for a child.

The twins were very different. Esau was "an outdoorsman who knew how to hunt, and Jacob became a quiet man who stayed at home" (Genesis 25:27). Not surprisingly, Isaac loved Esau; and Rebekah loved Jacob. When, in their adult life, Esau returned one evening from an unsuccessful hunt, he asked his younger brother for some of the stew he was boiling. Reading his brother's nature, Jacob said, "Sell me your birthright today" (25:31); and Esau, a man of compelling appetites, reasoned, "Since I'm going to die anyway, what good is my birthright to me?" (25:32). "He ate, drank, got up, and left" (25:34). Professor Alter comments, "This rapid-fire chain of verbs nicely expresses the precipitous manner in which Esau gulps down his food and, as the verse concludes, casts away his birthright."[2]

Genesis 26 is the one instance where we see Isaac acting for himself. It is difficult to say whether the events reported in this chapter are from an earlier period or are in sequence. We only know that there was a famine and that it was serious enough that Isaac thought of moving temporarily to Egypt. God instructed him to stay where he was. "I will keep my word, which I gave to your father Abraham. I will give you as many descendants as the stars in the sky, and I will give your descendants all of these lands. All of the nations of the earth will be blessed because of your descendants. I will do this because Abraham obeyed me" (Genesis 26:3-5).

Across the Testaments

Isaac Is Our Kin

Most New Testament references to Isaac are references to his genealogical place in history, but the apostle Paul relates him to believers as a symbol of faith. He explains in the Letter to the Galatians that although Abraham had two sons, the one [Ishmael] "was conceived the normal way," while the other [Isaac] "was conceived through a promise." "These things," Paul continues, "are an allegory"; and he wants his readers to understand, "you are the children of the promise like Isaac" (Galatians 4:23-24, 28). That is, we are children of faith, not of works or of ceremonial law.

Thus the earlier promise of God to Abraham (Genesis 12:1-3) was reaffirmed to Isaac. His own position continued to be rather passive. He was the carrier of the promise, yet it was his father's loyalty that was praised. God told Isaac that the blessing would come "because Abraham obeyed me and kept my orders" (26:5). This can be seen as belittling to Isaac. But one can also admire Isaac for being willing to fill his role and fill it well.

When Isaac went to Gerar to survive the period of famine, like Abraham he asked his wife to say that she was his sister so that his life would not be endangered. But King Abimelech saw familiarity between Isaac and Rebekah that was appropriate only for a husband and wife, and he realized they had lied. In spite of this act of deception, Isaac prospered greatly during his time in Gerar; and as Isaac and his company left Gerar, God "appeared to him that night" with reassurance regarding his role in the promise to Abraham (Genesis 26:24). "So Isaac built an altar there and worshipped in the LORD's name" (26:25). This is the only reference to Isaac building an altar. A tough-minded reader might reason that Isaac had seen enough of altars at Moriah.

The account of Isaac's duplicitous dealings in Gerar is not a pretty story, and it evokes two comments. For one, I marvel at the candor with which the Scriptures tell their story. There is no attempt to hide the failings of the biblical heroes or to explain or justify them. We're simply given the facts. I submit that the Bible is, indeed, an adult book, not because it treats matters salaciously, as does some contemporary reading and entertainment that is erroneously described as "adult," but because it asks us to respond like adults in our evaluating of our fellow human beings. Which is to say, we are to recognize that we humans are very human, made, as Genesis describes us, from the dust of the earth but, thanks be to God, also favored with the breath of God.

And a second comment. How is it that God blesses people who are as morally questionable as Isaac proves here to be and as Abraham was earlier in similar circumstances? Quite simply, God apparently has chosen to work with the stuff at hand. I have a feeling that Isaac was, so to speak, the best available at the time. And I remind myself that God has put up with me. (I won't speak for you.) I calculate that if we could see human beings as God does, in all our complexity, with our mixture of good intentions and marginal actions, and the thinking that goes into our words and deeds, we would realize that God is doing the best that can be done—the fairest and the most far-reaching—with what is at any moment part of the human story.

Isaac and His Sons

As Isaac grew old, his eyesight failed. One speculates that while the author is describing a physical condition, he is also suggesting a personality trait. In any event, when Isaac sent his favorite, Esau, to hunt and prepare some wild game in preparation for presenting Esau with his special blessing, Rebekah overheard the plan and immediately conspired with her favorite, Jacob, to deceive Isaac. We recall that Rebekah knew before the birth of her sons that the older would serve the younger. I think she reasoned that she would help bring God's purposes to pass, and I think she was wrong. But I've observed that now and again we try to "help" God by means that are not godly, arguing that the end justifies the means. We would do better to trust God—and especially, to work with God in ways consistent with godliness.

Jacob succeeded in the ruse, and thus Esau received only a secondary blessing. Esau, not surprisingly, "was furious at Jacob" (Genesis 27:41) and vowed that when the period of mourning for his father (whose death was thought to be imminent) was past, he would kill his brother.

Thus a family in which the ties had always been fragile was now broken. Jacob was forced to flee, but only after receiving a plea from his father to "marry one of the daughters of Laban, your mother's brother" (Genesis 28:2). Esau had already disappointed his parents by marrying Hittites (26:34-35). He now tried to remedy the situation by adding a wife from the family of Ishmael, his father's brother, who ironically was the other non-favored older brother (28:9). But despite this effort to marry within the family, Esau, like Ishmael, remained largely on the fringes of the family.

This stage of the family saga leaves the reader wondering if estrangement is the final word. But we'll discover in this instance as in so many others in Genesis that God is at work in the long haul, so to speak, ulti-mately bringing about reconciliation between brothers that at present seems impossible. Over twenty years later, Jacob and Esau were reconciled. Jacob eventually returned to see his father, and he and Esau buried him.

Live the Story

If you've read one of the occasional polls that give ratings to the great-ness of America's presidents, you may have noticed that the high rankings go to the presidents who led the nation during times of extreme stress, during war, economic depression, civic unrest. I submit that there is also greatness in holding a steady course in easier times. Indeed, perhaps we wouldn't have so many crises if we made better use of our more tran-quil days.

When you describe someone as a "godly person," do you make that judgment on the basis of their handling of a major illness or a family tragedy? Fine. But how about seeing the virtue in those persons who man-age, year after year, to do the good, the kind, the thoughtful, the generous thing, and who perhaps do it so naturally and unpretentiously that they go unnoticed.

I urge you to remember that God is at work in the slow scenes as well as in the tumultuous ones. While God didn't use Isaac in the same way as Abraham and Jacob, nevertheless God used him. So when the Scriptures use the phrase, "the God of Abraham, Isaac, and Jacob," Isaac's name gets the same inflection as the two more noticeable figures. There's something to be said for being good without being glamorous and for accomplishing without necessarily being noticed.

Do you feel that I'm making a case for mediocrity? I hope not, because as my students can tell you, I wage a continuing war against mediocrity. I think God will judge us for what we do with our gifts. This is the lesson, after all, in Jesus' parable of the talents (Matthew 25:14-30). In truth, I am making a case in vigorous support of what Jesus said. When we live in reasonably good times, or when we are blessed with health and favor, the temptation is to become comfortable and to "hide" our gift. The person with the one talent wasn't cursed for having only one talent but for failing to use what he had. I'm praising "Isaac" (any of you "Isaacs"!) for using your mind and heart and resources to meet the needs of your time, your place, and your opportunity, however large or small that opportunity may be.

1 From "Miniver Cheevy," by E.A. Robinson; see http://www.poemtree.com/poems/Miniver Cheevy.htm. (3-14-11)
2 From *The Five Books of Moses*, by Robert Alter (W.W. Norton, 2004); page 132.

7.

Jacob: The Making of a Patriarch

Genesis 28:10–36:8

Claim Your Story

You and I should walk carefully when we come to Jacob's story because his life is a minefield for the faith-explorer. We never know when we may step on something explosive. You already know that Jacob was one of Judaism's patriarchs, his name concluding that grand litany, "Abraham, Isaac, and Jacob." That alone puts him in select company.

But there's much more. Although Joseph occupies the single longest portion of the Book of Genesis and although Abraham is the key figure in the book, Jacob's life stretches over the largest portion of it. He enters at Genesis 25:26, and most of the closing chapter of Genesis (Chapter 50) is taken up with details of his burial. During Jacob's strategic meeting with God at the ford of the Jabbok (32:22-32), his name was changed to *Israel*. This is the name that exists today as the name of a country that plays a key role not only in the Middle East but also in the political and military affairs of the entire world.

Yet we wonder how Jacob gets his rank. When Abraham falters, still he towers over the scene. Although at times Isaac seems almost anonymous, he elicits our sympathy and at times our admiration. But Jacob? How is it that someone named "Heel-grabber" at birth (or "Supplanter," or even "Cheat," as some have named him) one day is christened "Prince" by God's order? Jacob is probably the most complex of the three patriarchs, and he is also the most unlikely.

Enter the Bible Story

As we noted earlier, when Rebekah experienced extraordinary discomfort during her pregnancy, God told her there were two nations in her womb and that the older would serve the younger—a violation of the legal codes of that time and still today in much of the world. Symbolically, when the twins emerged from the womb, Jacob's tiny, bloody hand was clutching the heel of his older brother, as if to declare that he was already pursuing his promised ascendancy.

A novelist might imagine how these brothers competed on the playing field or in the classroom, but in the Bible story they carried out their competition in very different domains: Esau as hunter and outdoorsman, cheered on by his father, and Jacob as student and homebody, beloved by his mother. You remember that sometime in their early manhood, Esau came home hungry; and Jacob played on his weakness and got Esau's birthright. That incident revealed the very different attitudes by which the two men lived. Esau's decisions were made for immediate gratification; Jacob had the long view. Jacob could wait.

We can excuse Jacob's conduct in this instance because while he did take advantage of his brother's weakness, Esau was old enough to know better. Yet in the next episode, when Jacob and his mother deceived his father in order to steal Esau's blessing, the best, poor excuse we can make for Jacob is that he was obeying his mother. But we have to add that Jacob, too, was old enough to know better. Now Jacob had to flee for his life, fearing his brother would kill him—a fear that still haunted Jacob twenty years later.

Jacob Met God

I wonder if Jacob had any misgivings as he left home. He was apparently a reluctant accomplice to his mother in deceiving his father and cheating his brother, but he persevered in lying to his father. His deed made him a fugitive from his own home. So he "set out for Haran" (Genesis 28:10), the city his grandfather had left so long before, and settled in for his first night's rest in some wilderness place. That night he saw a staircase reaching from earth to sky, with angels ascending and descending on it. Then God spoke. "I am the LORD, the God of your father Abraham and the God of Isaac" (28:13). Jacob wasn't told that his name would someday round out the phrase, but he received the promise that was given to Abraham and Isaac before him. More than that, he received an assurance for the immediate circumstances, one no doubt badly needed by this young man on the run. "I am with you now, I will protect you everywhere you go, and I will bring you back to this land. I will not leave you until I have done everything that I have promised you" (28:15). Have you had times when you wondered if you had wandered beyond God's jurisdiction, so to speak? What sign(s) did you see or experience that reassured you of God's presence even in a strange land?

Perhaps there was a bit of a spiritual genius in Jacob, in that he received the promise at a much earlier age than his father and grandfather. Or perhaps it was grace, God giving Jacob what at the moment he so desperately needed. Whatever, Jacob's response is fascinating. He recognized that God was "definitely in this place" (Genesis 28:16), and he was "terrified" (28:17). Jacob named the place Bethel, "God's house." But then he bargained with God the way he bargained with his brother when Esau came home hungry and smelled Jacob's soup. If God would protect him, Jacob offered, feed him and bring him back safely, then, he said, "the LORD

About the Christian Faith

Moving On Up

Until Jacob met God on his flight from home (Genesis 28:10-17), there was no evident godliness in his life. He was astute enough to want favors related to religion, including Esau's birthright and his blessing as the firstborn. But religion that is practiced only for benefit is no more than selfish superstition. When God was revealed to him at Bethel, however, Jacob experienced what might be called his conversion. But there had better be more. Faith begins at conversion, but it shouldn't end there. At a crisis some twenty years later, God reminded Jacob that they had met previously at Bethel (35:1). Remember your spiritual benchmarks, and use them to encourage your continuing faith journey.

will be my God" (28:21). He assured God further, "Of everything you give me I will give a tenth back to you" (28:22). As awestruck as Jacob was at Bethel, he managed to propose a very profitable deal with God.

Of course, Jacob wasn't the last to offer God such a deal. Athletes desperate to win, persons running for public office, executives hoping to close a merger, preachers dreaming of a better opportunity, romantics wanting to be loved in return—we are the children of Jacob, ready to give God a tenth if only God will give us much, much more.

Jacob Found a New Family

Jacob's search for a wife began at a watering place, just as did the search for Isaac's wife a generation earlier. This isn't surprising, since water was the key commodity in that place and time. Again, just the right person came along. Jacob had been instructed to "marry one of the daughters of Laban" (Genesis 28:2); and lo, a daughter of Laban came with her flocks. Furthermore, we learn that "she had a beautiful figure and was good-looking" (29:17). Jacob was properly smitten; and when his uncle suggested a month later that they have a remuneration agreement, Jacob knew just what he wanted: Rachel. He offered to work seven years to have her as his wife. Laban answered matter-of-factly, "I'd rather give her to you than to another man. Stay with me" (29:19). For Jacob, loving Rachel as he did, the seven years slipped by like a few days.

The contract was mutually beneficial. But a surprise awaited Jacob. A friend of mine notes that Laban and Jacob were "peas in a pod." If so, Uncle Laban was the older pea. The night of the wedding, after a great banquet, Laban substituted his older daughter, Leah, in the wedding tent. "In the morning, there she was—Leah!" (Genesis 29:25). When Jacob insisted he had been betrayed, Laban replied that in their culture the younger woman was not given before the firstborn. "Complete the celebratory week with this woman. Then I will give you this other woman too for your work, if you work for me seven more years" (29:27).

Of course Jacob accepted. What else could he do? How was he so deceived in the first place? Some classic rabbinical scholars say that the sisters were twins, the only difference being in their eyes—and no doubt in their manner. Remember that it was a world without artificial lighting; dark was dark! Remember, too, that the banqueting and the drinking that went with it could have made Jacob less than observant.

Whatever, a week later, Jacob had two wives—and the beginning of one of history's notably dysfunctional families. The biblical writer unfolds the story candidly: "Jacob slept with Rachel, and he loved Rachel more than Leah. . . . When the LORD saw that Leah was unloved, he opened her womb; but Rachel was unable to have children" (Genesis 29:30-31).

Leah bore Reuben ("see, a son"), Simeon (sounds like the Hebrew verb translated "hear"), Levi (sounds like the Hebrew verb translated "embrace"), and Judah (sounds like the Hebrew verb translated "praise") in what was probably rather rapid succession. There is pathos in the names Leah gives to these sons; the meaning of the names is an emotional and spiritual biography of a used and rejected woman. I marvel at Leah's insistent faith and good cheer. I wish I were a novelist so I could tell her story. Meanwhile, "Rachel became jealous of her sister," so jealous that she told Jacob, "I may as well be dead" (Genesis 30:1). Jacob didn't take this well ("Do you think I'm God?" [30:2].). Rachel had Jacob sleep with her servant girl, Bilhah, bringing Dan ("he judged") into the family and then Naphtali ("my competition" or "my wrestling"). At this point Leah offered her servant girl, Zilpah, to whom Gad ("good fortune") was born and then Asher ("happy"). Leah then had two more sons of her own; and again they were given optimistic names, Issachar ("there is payment") and Zebulon ("honor"). She also had a daughter, Dinah. Only then, at last, did Rachel conceive and bear her first child. "She named him Joseph [meaning "he adds"], saying to herself, May the LORD give me another son" (30:24). When that son, Benjamin, came several years later, Rachel died in childbirth. He was the last child to be born into the family.

Jacob complained later that Laban changed his salary "ten times" (Genesis 31:7), but an increasingly clever Jacob found ways to build a substantial fortune. Of course, this strained Jacob's relationship with Laban and with Laban's sons, who saw the family wealth being diluted to their brother-in-law, whose cleverness wasn't winsome to in-laws who realized their economic future was disappearing. Jacob knew it was time to leave.

It wasn't a pleasant break; but warned of God not to touch Jacob, Laban sent him and his household on their way. Jacob was escaping a crisis, but the most important elements in his story were still ahead.

Jacob Met God, and Esau

Thus far we haven't seen much in Jacob to qualify him as a patriarch in a divine movement. Except for the night that began his pilgrimage at Bethel, Jacob's biography has been that of a very clever entrepreneur, a man with a gift for making much out of almost nothing—and also a rather frazzled family man. But as he terminated his ties with Laban, Jacob met God anew (Genesis 32:1-2), apparently in preparation for a meeting with his estranged brother, Esau.

Jacob was still the astute business negotiator. He sent a preliminary message to Esau briefly relating his success but concluding, "I'm sending this message to my master now to ask that he be kind" (Genesis 32:5). Jacob's messenger returned with bad news. Esau was coming to meet him with four hundred men. "Jacob," Genesis tells us, "was terrified and felt trapped" (32:7). There was a lot of wilderness out there, but there was no place to hide—not when you were traveling with all your possessions and your family.

So Jacob continued in the ways he knew best, organizing his resources and his family in a fashion calculated to win if possible but at worst to lose expediently. The Scriptures report, "Jacob thought, I may be able to pacify Esau with the gift I'm sending ahead. When I meet him, perhaps he will be kind to me" (Genesis 32:20). "Jacob sent the gift ahead . . . , but he spent that night in the camp" (32:21).

We sense that Jacob couldn't sleep. He got up, awakened Leah and Rachel and their maidservants and the children, and "crossed the Jabbok River's shallow water" (Genesis 32:22). Still, no rest. Alone, terribly alone, he was joined by "a man" who wrestled with him, wrestled, indeed, "until dawn broke" (32:24). The midnight stranger "saw that he couldn't defeat Jacob," so he "tore a muscle in Jacob's thigh" as they wrestled (32:25). But Jacob—still the heel-grabber, still the one who could foil his older brother and his father-in-law—wouldn't let go. He sensed that his wrestler was not simply a nighttime hoodlum but someone with divine connection. "I won't let you go," Jacob said, "until you bless me" (32:26).

But first the stranger asked Jacob to tell him his name. Any really crucial encounter with God includes a moment when we face who we are. Jacob's name had a mystical quality, one that marked him from his birth. He had fulfilled its description through youth and manhood, at home and in business. Now he must acknowledge the dark side of that name. And when he did, the stranger gave him a new name: Israel.

Jacob wasn't done. He wanted to know the name of the stranger with whom he had been in such a fierce, night-long embrace. The stranger brushed aside Jacob's question.

So who was it with whom Jacob wrestled that night? A poet might say that Jacob was wrestling with himself—with his past, his misshapen ambitions, his fear of the postponed showdown with his brother. A theologian might say that Jacob wrestled with the Holy Spirit, as all of us sinners must do if we are to be changed. Jacob himself was satisfied even though he did not receive an answer. "I've seen God face-to-face, and my life has been saved" (Genesis 32:30). Charles Wesley, the cofounder of the Methodist movement, saw Jacob's encounter as a picture of his own meeting with God and told the story in fourteen moving stanzas. When the stranger refuses to speak his name, Charles Wesley answers with assurance,

> 'Tis Love! 'tis Love! thou diedst for me,
> I hear thy whisper in my heart. . . .
> Thy nature, and thy name is Love.[1]

Having done business with God, Jacob's meeting with Esau was a kind of anticlimax. But the marvel is this, that Esau—the one not chosen—is the voice of grace and of reconciliation. It almost gives one pause about how God may be working in our time, outside as well as inside the church, to accomplish God's aims. The careful language of Genesis makes clear the connection between Jacob's two encounters. Jacob left Peniel saying, "I've seen God face-to-face" (Genesis 32:30); now he told Esau, "Seeing your face is like seeing God's face" (33:10). The two brothers went their separate ways, apparently not to meet again until at the time of Isaac's death.

Jacob's Continuing Journey

The years that followed in Jacob's life were irregular. There is the sorry story of Dinah and Shechem, in which Jacob's sons Simeon and Levi ignored Jacob's counsel and exacted a terrible revenge (Genesis 34).Then we have Benjamin's birth (35:16-18), Rachel's death (35:19), Isaac's death (35:27-29), and a chapter detailing Esau's family (Genesis 36).

Then the story focuses on Joseph, Jacob's favorite and favored son, until Jacob himself becomes almost a bit player in the drama. Jacob made it easy for his older sons to resent Joseph and then seek to remove him from the family by selling him into slavery while letting Jacob think the boy had been killed by a wild animal. Jacob eventually learned not only that Joseph was still alive, but that he was now second only to the king in Egypt, a man whose judgments determined what food would be given to surrounding nations during a wide famine.

The family was reunited in Egypt, and Jacob saw the son whose prowess he had honored prematurely with a ceremonial robe now wearing imperial garments. Almost all of Genesis 49 is a record of Jacob's last words to his sons, blessings, and predictions. In the closing chapter of Genesis, we see the family burying Jacob in the site that Abraham bought generations earlier, where Abraham, Sarah, Isaac, Rebekah, and Leah were buried. Jacob has completed his pilgrimage. He has not been a perfect man

---

Across the Testaments

Jacob as Patriarch

Jacob gets his place in the closing chapters of the New Testament just as he does at the end of Genesis. As John the Revelator sees the Holy City, among the special wonders of the city are the twelve jeweled gates. And how are they identified? They bear "the names of the twelve tribes of Israel's sons" (Revelation 21:12). It is, fittingly, Jacob's redeemed name, Israel, that carries into the Holy City.

(Who is?). Sometimes it's been difficult to like him. But he has had his grand moments, especially in the dark night when he wrestled with God and with his own soul and won by being defeated.

Live the Story

In a perverse sort of way I am always encouraged by Jacob's story. I said a moment ago that at times he was hard to like, but in total I would love to have known him. For sure, a friendship with Jacob would never have been dull.

But why did God use Jacob, and what can we learn from him? At the level of his talents, Jacob was the kind of person who would succeed in any time or place. He was bright; was a quick learner; and had good people skills (except at times within his own family) and a creative, entrepreneurial mind.

Far more important, Jacob had a mind for God. He valued what was spiritual in his culture: his birthright and a unique blessing. It seems that these matters were incidental to Esau. Jacob knew how to respond to a vision at Bethel; and although his response was marked by self-serving, it was also marked by a very real, very intense worship. In the night at the Jabbok Brook, he held on with the tenacity that one finds in the stories of all the great saints, whether in Judaism or Christianity. When we hear him say, "I won't let you go until you bless me" (Genesis 32:26), we know all we need to know about what made Jacob special. One must prize God and a relationship with God above all else if one is to climb the heights of the spirit.

How does the story of Jacob's wrestling with God resonate with your experience? When have you had times of anxiety and painful struggle with God? Did those struggles eventually lead to a blessing, to some positive outcome? Could you have had the blessing without the struggle?

---

1 From "Come, O Thou Traveler Unknown," by Charles Wesley, in *The United Methodist Hymnal* (Copyright © 1989 by The United Methodist Publishing House); 387.

8.

Joseph's Place in the Big Story

Genesis 37–50

Claim Your Story

If your Sunday school experience was anything like mine, you heard a lot about Joseph. He was a made-to-order hero and example, not simply because he came out a winner, but because he had to deal with so many crises and rejections to get there.

As you read Joseph's story, you may discover that you are reliving chapters in your own life. Have siblings or members of your extended family turned against you, perhaps envying some true or imaginary privilege that has come your way? Have you lost a job or a promotion or a friendship because you've tried to hold on to your integrity? Have circumstances, perhaps even death, cut you off from the people you love most? And have you had to wait for what seemed a very long time for things to work out right? If so, Joseph will seem like an old friend.

Of course, there's more to Joseph's story. He is a major element in the biblical plot, so much so that we're given more details of his life than of any other Genesis character. He is a study in Divine Providence.

But what, exactly, is "Providence"; and what does it mean in your life or in your mind? What role is God playing in your life? And what part might you be playing in some of the larger stories of family; neighborhood; workplace; church; or, well, who knows how far?

Enter the Bible Story

Like Isaac and Jacob before him, Joseph was a long-awaited child, born to a mother who was thought to be unable to conceive and seen therefore not only as a particular joy but also as an answer to prayer. You remember that Jacob was maneuvered into marrying two sisters, one of whom (Leah) bore him a number of children, while Rachel, whom he so deeply loved, could not conceive. Eventually, Rachel became pregnant with Joseph. "God has taken away my shame," she declared (Genesis 30:23).

Joseph's Unique Relationship to Jacob

Genesis tells us that "Israel loved Joseph more than any of his other sons because he was born when Jacob was old" (Genesis 37:3). This is a strange line, since Joseph's younger brother, Benjamin, was born when Jacob was even older and both had Rachel, Jacob's favorite wife, as their mother.

But there is more. I quote from the Alter translation: "This is the lineage of Jacob—Joseph, seventeen years old, was tending the flock with his brothers, assisting the sons of Bilhah and the sons of Zilpah, the wives of his father."[1] If the writer is giving us the "lineage of Jacob," we expect that he will begin with Reuben, the firstborn, or perhaps by listing all of Jacob's sons; certainly we don't expect that he will choose to name the eleventh son.

What is Genesis telling us? It is telling us that the story of Jacob, as unfolded through his sons, is going to unfold specifically through Joseph. To put it in the language of a novelist, Joseph is the plot line. Some rabbinical scholars suggest that the writer of Genesis is telling us that Joseph was Jacob's *spiritual* heir; that while he was not physically or legally the firstborn, he was the one whom Jacob knew as his true heir, the one who carried on the quality in the family line that mattered most to Jacob. I can imagine Jacob saying, as he looked at his sons, "The rest of them look like their Uncle Esau!"

So without further evidence of Joseph's merit, his father gave him a special coat. The Hebrew is obscure; the familiar phrase is "a coat of many colors." Others call it "an ankle-length coat," still others "a coat with sleeves." Whatever, it wasn't something made by one of the family maids. It was meant to distinguish Joseph from his brothers, which, of course, didn't endear him to them.

Beautiful coat or not, Joseph had to work in the family business. He began humbly, watching herds with the sons of the handmaidens. When he returned from this assignment, "Joseph told their father unflattering things about them" (Genesis 37:2). In common parlance, Joseph was a snitch. Worse, Joseph dreamed; and he told his dreams. The first dream was of a day when the brothers were binding stalks in a field. Suddenly, Joseph's stalk stood upright; and the other stalks bowed down to his. The brothers got the point: Joseph dreamed of ruling over them. A second dream had the sun, moon, and eleven stars doing obeisance to him, as if even his parents would pay him honor. Some dreams we should keep to ourselves. If we do not, this shows that we may be precociously bright yet lack basic common sense. No wonder Joseph's brothers hated him so much that they "couldn't even talk nicely to him" (37:4). Joseph's father reprimanded him gently but "took careful note" of what the boy had said (37:11).

The Brothers Get Revenge

Seething anger will eventually find an outlet. Joseph was now working out of the home office, while the older brothers were watching the flocks near Shechem. One day Jacob said, "Go! Find out how your brothers are and how the flock is, and report back to me" (Genesis 37:14). When the brothers saw him coming ("Here comes the big dreamer" [Genesis 37:19].), they agreed to kill him, throw his body into a cistern, and tell their father that a wild animal had devoured him.

I submit that if they had carried out this plan, there would not be a nation of Israel today and that the Bible story would be a quite different one.

Reuben interceded, however. Hoping he could eventually save Joseph's life, Reuben suggested that they put him in a cistern for the time being. So, "they stripped off Joseph's long robe" (Genesis 37:23)—a telling detail on the writer's part—and threw him in the cistern. Then, as they were eating, a trader's caravan came by; and Judah noted that there was no gain in killing their brother. Why not sell him into slavery and make a profit while also getting rid of him? They did so, then dipped Joseph's robe in the blood of a male goat and returned to their father. Jacob assumed that Joseph had been killed. He "tore his clothes" (37:34) and entered a period of mourning, a period that lasted ceremonially for the usual time but that continued in fact for many years, until he learned that Joseph was still alive. Jacob's obvious favoritism was grievous, and he paid for it grievously.

Joseph as Slave and Prisoner

Joseph was sold into the household of Potiphar, commander of Pharaoh's royal guard. The writer of Genesis tells us, "The LORD was with Joseph, and he became a successful man and served in his Egyptian master's household" (Genesis 39:2). "Successful man" is an interesting description for a servant—actually, a slave. It reminds us that most of our definitions of "success," while attempting to be big, are usually too small. Potiphar saw that God's blessing was on Joseph and thought so highly of him that he made him his assistant, head of his household.

Success is a perilous platform, however. "Joseph was well-built and handsome" (Genesis 39:6); and as time went by, Potiphar's wife began to notice him and then set out to seduce him. "Every single day she tried to convince him" (39:10), and Joseph refused with a straightforward argument: his loyalty to his employer and his divine responsibility. "How could I do this terrible thing and sin against God?" (39:9). But one fateful day Potiphar's wife pulled Joseph's garment from him (painfully reminiscent of his brothers' actions at a cistern near Dothan) as Joseph fled from her appeals. She then summoned other servants to tell them that Joseph had tried to assault her. When she gave the report to Potiphar that evening, "he was incensed" (39:19) and threw Joseph in jail. Let me pause to say that Joseph's story is a story of God's Providence at work, and God's Providence uses every kind of material in building its projects. An ugly stone may be as propitious as a jewel.

About the Christian Faith

The Role of Providence

Our ancestors spoke of Providence more than we do. Perhaps they over spoke; we don't pay enough attention to it. The writer of Genesis makes clear that God is at work in our individual lives and in larger moments of history. William Cowper, the eighteenth-century poet, warned that "blind unbelief is sure to err, / And scan [God's] work in vain." He urged a better faith in Providence: "God is his own interpreter, / And he will make it plain."[2]

Among other things, this jail was a more-than-ordinary jail; it was "the place where the king's prisoners were held" (Genesis 39:20). Here, again, Joseph's integrity and managerial skills were recognized and rewarded. More than that, "the LORD was with Joseph and remained loyal to him" (39:21); the Lord was no fair weather friend. In time the jail's commander put all the prisoners under Joseph's supervision. "The jail's commander paid no attention to anything under Joseph's supervision, because the LORD was with him and made everything he did successful" (39:23).

New prisoners came one day from the ranks of those closest to the king, closer even than some of his political and military advisers: his wine steward and his baker. These men, you see, were the persons who, if disloyal, could work with the king's enemies to bring about the king's death. These two trusted officials had come into disrepute and were now in prison. Joseph found himself overseeing two significant though deposed officers. Call it an opportunity for Providence.

One night both men dreamed—dreams that upset them because they were too precise to seem ordinary. Joseph, a sensitive young man, inquired into their distress. When they referred to their dreams, he made a witness typical of him: "Don't interpretations belong to God? Describe your dreams to me" (Genesis 40:8). The wine steward's dream, Joseph explained, was a favorable one. In three days he would be restored to his former position. Unfortunately for the baker, in three days he would be executed.

The Two Josephs

The Joseph of Genesis is known for his dreams, first about himself and then the dreams of the baker, the wine steward, and Pharaoh. The Joseph of the Gospel of Matthew was an even greater dreamer, though his dreams were restricted to a shorter period of time and to his private experience. An angel came to him in a dream to reassure him regarding his marriage to Mary and to instruct him regarding the naming of Jesus (Matthew 1:18-25). Then an angel appeared in a dream to tell Joseph to take the Holy Family to Egypt, to escape Herod's wrath (2:13-15). After Herod's death, an angel again came in a dream to report that Herod was dead and to tell Joseph the family could return (2:19-20). The angel came again to tell Joseph to settle in Galilee rather than in Judea (2:22-23).

When Joseph interpreted the steward's dream, he added a personal appeal: "But please, remember me when you are doing well and be loyal to me. Put in a good word for me to Pharaoh, so he sets me free from this prison" (Genesis 40:14). In three days the dreams of both men were fulfilled—tragically for the baker and beautifully for the steward. "But the chief wine steward didn't remember Joseph; he forgot all about him" (40:23).

Joseph as Prime Minister

In the ways of Providence, even poor memories sometimes serve a purpose. If the wine steward had given Pharaoh information about Joseph, it would shortly have been lost in the executive files because information not needed is usually information discarded. Two full years passed. You and I can imagine Joseph's state of mind during that period. I venture that Joseph began waiting for word from the steward or Pharaoh the day after the steward's release because most of us are inclined to feel that our concerns are as important to others as they are to us. Then he argued with himself that it would take a week or two. Or a month. Or—well, the wise man said, "Hope deferred maketh the heart sick" (Proverbs 13:12, KJV). I think Joseph got a sick heart, then buried his dream in realism. He would never hear from his once-friend, the wine steward.

But Providence works within the boundaries of human events—our politics and economics and personal peculiarities. One night Pharaoh had a dream. In fact, he had two dreams, but with striking similarities. Pharaoh was mightily disturbed, and none of his religious experts could help him. Then the steward's faulty memory recovered. "Today," he told Pharaoh, "I've just remembered my mistake" (Genesis 41:9). At this moment I want to say, "Well, it's about time!" And Providence answers, "Exactly. Now it's time."

Suddenly, Joseph was not only the dream interpreter to Pharaoh; he was in effect the prime minister of Egypt. Thirteen years had passed since Joseph was sold into slavery. He was now thirty years old, and he sat at the right hand of the most powerful man of his time. He was arbiter now of Egypt's major industry, agriculture, and with it of Egypt's eventual social welfare. In time he would be the key figure in Egypt's international relations, when Egypt became the source of food for surrounding nations.

Joseph as Son and Sibling

Joseph's success was a means to an end, not an end in itself. He had an extended family back in his homeland, a family called to carry on the promise made to Abraham, Isaac, and Jacob.

The famine eventually brought them to Egypt. Joseph recognized his older brothers; but, of course, they didn't recognize him: a grown man of supreme authority and magisterial bearing, with Egyptian tonsure, elegant garments. He had no resemblance to the seventeen-year-old they pulled from a cistern and sent half-naked into slavery. Joseph played the situation to its dramatic hilt in a series of episodes. But he realized that God had used the events of the past. "I'm your brother Joseph! The one you sold to Egypt. . . . Actually, God sent me before you to save lives" (Genesis 45:4-5).

With Pharaoh's favor, Joseph was able to bring his extended family to Egypt, a move that God endorsed for Jacob in a renewal of the promise. Genesis tells us that the family of Jacob (including Joseph, his wife, and two sons) totaled seventy, a multiple of the number seven, the Hebrew symbol of completeness. Jacob was able not only to see Joseph's success and to bless his sons, Ephraim and Manasseh, but to claim those sons as his own. Before his death, Jacob assembled his sons to tell them "what will happen to you in the coming days" (Genesis 49:1).

Following Jacob's death and his burial in Canaan, Joseph's older brothers feared that with their father gone, Joseph would bear a grudge and would pay them back "seriously" for what they did to him (Genesis 50:15). But when they made their apology and their appeal ("We're here as your slaves" [50:18].), Joseph answered as their brother and as an interpreter of the purposes of God. "You planned something bad for me, but God produced something good from it, in order to save the lives of many people, just as he's doing today" (50:20).

So we see that Joseph was much more than a skilled administrator and certainly more than the bright teenager on whom his father doted. He proved to be the unifier of a family almost doomed to dysfunction by its origins. When one ponders the household that began with Jacob, Leah, and Rachel, one wonders how peace could ever come to pass. In a peculiar way, Joseph brought to center stage his erratic but sensitive older brother, Judah. Judah's first recorded speech is the recommendation to his brothers that instead of killing Joseph, they sell him to the Ishmaelite caravan, which then delivered him to Egypt (Genesis 37:25-28). All the rest of the plot depended on this.

No wonder, then, that the account of Judah's transgression with his daughter-in-law, Tamar, comes as an interruption in the Joseph story (Genesis 38), introduced by the phrase, "At that time," that is, a story that unfolds over at least twenty years but that is background or foreground to the larger story of Joseph. It was Judah who persuaded his father to allow Benjamin to join the second trip to Egypt (43:1-15). And it was Judah who made the impassioned speech to Joseph on behalf of Benjamin and his father (one of the longest speeches in Genesis), a speech that brought Joseph to his self-revealing (44:18–45:3). Judah was eventually the major tribe in Israel, the tribe from which their greatest king, David, came, and, for Christians, the line from which Jesus was born (Matthew 1:2).

Judah, I repeat, comes on stage via the Joseph story. And it was by Joseph that Israel came to Egypt where in time they became slaves.

Without the isolation and unification that came from their slavery, one doubts that Israel would have become a nation—a nation that exists and influences history to the present day, long after the Jebusites, Ammonites, and Hittites are historical bypaths.

Live the Story

Although Joseph is not included with "Abraham, Isaac, and Jacob" in the iconic formula, it's clear that the story would have died with Jacob if it hadn't been for Joseph. As our childhood teachers told us, Joseph is an example of steadfast character, unafraid to confess his trust in God; but he is more.

Joseph realized a crucial truth about himself: He was to be in place so God could use him in matters beyond himself. Joseph believed in Providence, the conviction that God is at work in our world and that God can use circumstances good and bad to bring the divine will to pass. Joseph was pleased to be God's instrument regardless of the personal cost.

You and I never know how God might use us. Especially, you may not realize that God *desires* to use you. The secret is in our being willing. This means trusting God, no matter what our particular circumstances.

Wendell Berry, the remarkable poet and novelist who still works his farm with a horse and a hand-held plow, says that you and I are "travelers, walking to the sun." We don't do well at seeing ahead, "but looking back the very light / That blinded us shows us the way we came."[3] That, I think, is Providence. Frederick Buechner, another poet and novelist, says that "Christians are people who . . . through Christ, have been delivered just enough to know that there's more where that came from."[4] That is, we see just enough of Providence in our past to have confidence for today and tomorrow—Divine Providence.

1 From *The Five Books of Moses*, by Robert Alter (W.W. Norton, 2004); page 206.

2 From "God Moves in a Mysterious Way," by William Cowper, in *The Methodist Hymnal* (Copyright © 1964, 1966 by Board of Publication of The Methodist Church, Inc.); 215.

3 From *Given*, by Wendell Berry (Shoemaker Hoard, 2005); page 74.

4 From *A Room Called Remember*, by Frederick Buechner (Harper & Row, 1984); page 112.

Leader Guide

People often view the Bible as a maze of obscure people, places, and events from centuries ago and struggle to relate it to their daily lives. IMMERSION invites us to experience the Bible as a record of God's loving revelation to humankind. These studies recognize our emotional, spiritual, and intellectual needs and welcome us into the Bible story and into deeper faith.

As leader of an IMMERSION group, you will help participants to encounter the Word of God and the God of the Word that will lead to new creation in Christ. You do not have to be an expert to lead; in fact, you will participate with your group in listening to and applying God's life-transforming Word to your lives. You and your group will explore the building blocks of the Christian faith through key stories, people, ideas, and teachings in every book of the Bible. You will also explore the bridges and points of connection between the Old and New Testaments.

Choosing and Using the Bible

The central goal of IMMERSION is engaging the members of your group with the Bible in a way that informs their minds, forms their hearts, and transforms the way they live out their Christian faith. Participants will need this study book and a Bible. IMMERSION is an excellent accompaniment to the Common English Bible (CEB). It shares with the CEB four common aims: clarity of language, faith in the Bible's power to transform lives, the emotional expectation that people will find the love of God, and the rational expectation that people will find the knowledge of God.

Other recommended study Bibles include *The New Interpreter's Study Bible* (NRSV), *The New Oxford Annotated Study Bible* (NRSV), *The HarperCollins Study Bible* (NRSV), the *NIV and TNIV Study Bibles*, and the *Archaeological Study Bible* (NIV). Encourage participants to use more than one translation. *The Message: The Bible in Contemporary Language* is a modern paraphrase of the Bible, based on the original languages. Eugene H. Peterson has created a masterful presentation of the Scripture text, which is best used alongside rather than in place of the CEB or another primary English translation.

One of the most reliable interpreters of the Bible's meaning is the Bible itself. Invite participants first of all to allow Scripture to have its say. Pay attention to context. Ask questions of the text. Read every passage with curiosity, always seeking to answer the basic Who? What? Where? When? and Why? questions.

Bible study groups should also have handy essential reference resources in case someone wants more information or needs clarification on specific words, terms, concepts, places, or people mentioned in the Bible. A Bible dictionary, Bible atlas, concordance, and one-volume Bible commentary together make for a good, basic reference library.

The Leader's Role

An effective leader prepares ahead. This leader guide provides easy to follow, step-by-step suggestions for leading a group. The key task of the leader is to guide discussion and activities that will engage heart and head and will invite faith development. Discussion questions are included, and you may want to add questions posed by you or your group. Here are suggestions for helping your group engage Scripture:

State questions clearly and simply.

Ask questions that move Bible truths from "outside" (dealing with concepts, ideas, or information about a passage) to "inside" (relating to the experiences, hopes, and dreams of the participants).

Work for variety in your questions, including compare and contrast, information recall, motivation, connections, speculation, and evaluation.

Avoid questions that call for yes-or-no responses or answers that are obvious.

Don't be afraid of silence during a discussion. It often yields especially thoughtful comments.

Test questions before using them by attempting to answer them yourself.

When leading a discussion, pay attention to the mood of your group by "listening" with your eyes as well as your ears.

Guidelines for the Group

IMMERSION is designed to promote full engagement with the Bible for the purpose of growing faith and building up Christian community. While much can be gained from individual reading, a group Bible study offers an ideal setting in which to achieve these aims. Encourage participants to bring their Bibles and read from Scripture during the session. Invite participants to consider the following guidelines as they participate in the group:

Respect differences of interpretation and understanding.

Support one another with Christian kindness, compassion, and courtesy.

Listen to others with the goal of understanding rather than agreeing or disagreeing.

Celebrate the opportunity to grow in faith through Bible study.

Approach the Bible as a dialogue partner, open to the possibility of being challenged or changed by God's Word.

Recognize that each person brings unique and valuable life experiences to the group and is an important part of the community.

Reflect theologically—that is, be attentive to three basic questions: What does this say about God? What does this say about me/us? What does this say about the relationship between God and me/us?

Commit to a lived faith response in light of insights you gain from the Bible. In other words, what changes in attitudes (how you believe) or actions (how you behave) are called for by God's Word?

Group Sessions

The group sessions, like the chapters themselves, are built around three sections: "Claim Your Story," "Enter the Bible Story," and "Live the Story." Sessions are designed to move participants from an awareness of their own life story, issues, needs, and experiences into an encounter and dialogue with the story of Scripture and to make decisions integrating their personal stories and the Bible's story.

The session plans in the following pages will provide questions and activities to help your group focus on the particular content of each chapter. In addition to questions and activities, the plans will include chapter title, Scripture, and faith focus.

Here are things to keep in mind for all the sessions:

Prepare Ahead
Study the Scripture, comparing different translations and perhaps a paraphrase.
Read the chapter, and consider what it says about your life and the Scripture.
Gather materials such as large sheets of paper or a markerboard with markers.
Prepare the learning area. Write the faith focus for all to see.

Welcome Participants
Invite participants to greet one another.
Tell them to find one or two people and talk about the faith focus.
Ask: What words stand out for you? Why?

Guide the Session
Look together at "Claim Your Story." Ask participants to give their reactions to the stories and examples given in each chapter. Use questions from the session plan to elicit comments based on personal experiences and insights.

Ask participants to open their Bibles and "Enter the Bible Story." For each portion of Scripture, use questions from the session plan to help participants gain insight into the text and relate it to issues in their own lives.

Step through the activity or questions posed in "Live the Story." Encourage participants to embrace what they have learned and to apply it in their daily lives.

Invite participants to offer their responses or insights about the boxed material in "Across the Testaments," "About the Scripture," and "About the Christian Faith."

Close the Session
Encourage participants to read the following week's Scripture and chapter before the next session.
Offer a closing prayer.

1. How It All Began
Genesis 1–2

Faith Focus

Human beings—men and women as equal partners—are made in the image of God and entrusted to care responsibly for the marvelous and good world that God has created.

Before the Session

Here's a big assignment: If you possibly can, read the entire Book of Genesis, preferably at a single sitting. Confused about some of the things you read? Fine. Read those passages in several different translations. Make a list of the questions you have about Genesis as you read through the book; most likely these will be the same questions your group members will raise as they study this ancient and fascinating book.

Second, jot down some of the things you've heard about the Book of Genesis or some of the conflicts surrounding this book. For example, the conflict between those who believe in what has come to be called "Creationism" and those who believe in evolution becomes heated from time to time as some argue for the inclusion of both ideas in school textbooks.

Again, the questions and concerns you bring to this book will mirror the concerns and questions the members of your group will bring.

Claim Your Story

Begin this session by asking group members to work in teams of three to identify the differences they note between Genesis 1–2:4a and Genesis 2:4b-25. What questions and concerns do these seemingly two different accounts of Creation raise in the minds of the team members? For example, did God create men and women at the same time, as in the first account of Creation; or did God create a man first, then a woman from the man, as in the second account. Don't expect perfectly clear answers to questions such as these. Genesis is a very ancient book that does not lend itself to neat and precise answers.

Reassemble as a whole group. If some of the teams have "burning questions," hear these and post them on a chalkboard or large sheet of paper for consideration during the rest of the session.

Enter the Bible Story
A Very Personal Book

Divide your group into teams of three again, preferably not the same three in each team as before. Ask each team of three to discuss this question: What feeling or impression regarding the Book of Genesis did you form from reading the words of Dr. Kalas (the writer of the study) regarding Genesis 1 and 2? How does Dr. Kalas approach these two chapters that begin the Book of Genesis? What does this say about the way we ought to approach the Book of Genesis? Hear reports from several of the teams. Help the whole group recognize that Dr. Kalas approaches Genesis as a very personal and almost intimate book. He does not view it as an academic study or as a puzzle to be solved; instead, Dr. Kalas reveals that he reads Genesis in a very personal, up close way. Ask for some examples of this from the section of the study entitled "Enter the Bible Story." How does Dr. Kalas' approach differ from the ways in which most of us approach the Book of Genesis? What does Dr. Kalas' approach say to us? How does his approach speak to some of the questions regarding the differences between Chapters 1 and 2 of Genesis? Hear ideas from several group members.

God's Perfect Light and God's Creative Word

Dr. Kalas emphasizes (among other things) two aspects of Creation. One is God's first command: "Let there be light" (Genesis 1:3). The second is the ways in which God pronounced all things into being. What does the story of God calling all things into being by the power of God's spoken word say to us in our day and time? What does it say about God and who God is?

Note in Genesis 1 that the first commandment God gives is that light appear. What does light symbolize to you? What does the absence of light suggest or symbolize? Note that the light that God calls into being is not the light of the sun, moon, or stars; these come later. According to some traditions, this is the same light that the apostles beheld at Jesus' transfiguration, the same light that illuminated Moses' face as he came down from his mountaintop meeting with God.

Ask: What can we conclude about God from God's perfect light and God's creative Word?

God Declares Creation Good

A third aspect of Creation that Dr. Kalas emphasizes is God's declaration that each created thing is "good." What attributes must something have to be declared "good" by almighty God? If God has declared something "good," what should be our reaction or response to that something? Use these questions to lead into a brief discussion of our responsibility toward all created things. Are we as human beings acting as good stewards of all that God declared good? What might God be saying in including humankind within all that God declares as "good"?

Live the Story

Ask group members to ponder this question in silence: What does the Creation story in the Book of Genesis call me to be and to do?

Then close with a brief prayer of thanksgiving for all of God's creation.

2. The Beginnings of Sin and of Grace
Genesis 3:1–4:17, 25

Faith Focus

God desires fellowship with human beings and shalom (right relationships) for all. But human beings have a propensity to misuse freedom, resulting in alienation from God, from each other, and from all creation.

Before the Session

Again, read the passages covered in this chapter of the study (Genesis 3:1–4:17, 25) in as many translations as you can find. Then, for yourself, try to write out a definition of sin. Is sin defined as individual acts that we do? Or is sin a relationship—or lack of a relationship? Think carefully: What caused the sin in both of the cases in this passage, the sin of Eve and Adam and the sin of Cain? What human characteristic led to the sin in both cases? Is that human characteristic still among us today? If so, how can we deal with it and how can we overcome it?

As always, be prepared to help group members look beyond the stories to the reality that the stories represent. Don't get hung up on, for example, whether or not snakes can talk or other such details.

Gather slips of paper and pencils for each group member.

Claim Your Story

Ask the group members to form pairs—not wives with husbands, if possible—and discuss some of these questions: What is sin? Does sin always have consequences? Are these consequences always immediate? Give examples of your responses. Secondly, what causes sin? What caused the sin of Adam and Eve and the sin of Cain? Would Adam and Eve have sinned without the snake? Why do you answer as you do? What does the snake represent in the story of Adam and Eve? Is the human characteristic that caused these sins still rife today? If so, in what ways and in what forms?

Reassemble as a whole group and let those pairs who wish to do so share some of their conversations.

Enter the Bible Story

Sin as Believing in Something Other Than God

Ask group members to review quickly the first six paragraphs in the section of this chapter in the study titled "Enter the Bible Story." How does Dr. Kalas (the writer of the study) define the sin of Adam and Eve? Adam and Eve chose to hear and obey the voice of the intruder rather than the voice of God. Do we do the same? If so, who or what is the "intruder" in our day and age? Think carefully: Is the intruder always outside of us, beyond us, apart from us? How, when, and in what ways does the intruder live within us?

Consequences of Human Disobedience

Reflect as a whole group on Dr. Kalas' comments about Adam and Eve's decision to make garments for themselves. Nakedness suggests vulnerability; Adam and Eve felt vulnerable, including vulnerable to God's judgment and punishment. While fig leaf garments would not protect them, at least the fig leaves reduced the feelings of vulnerability just a bit. Ask group members to talk in threes about times they have felt especially vulnerable, that is, capable of being hurt deeply in many different ways. Is a sense of vulnerability always a consequence of sin? Why do you answer as you do?

Dr. Kalas indicates that the question God asked of Adam and Eve ("Where are you?") is the basic theological question. For until we can confess that we are in sin, we can find no way out of that sin. But what did Adam and Eve do? Discuss as a whole group the response the pair made to God's question. What human characteristic is displayed by their answers?

Cain and Abel

As a whole group, review quickly the story of Cain and Abel. What caused the sin of Cain? Is that cause still rampant in our world today? If so, how?

God's Gracious Response to Sin

But—and with God there is always the divine "but"—what was God's response to both the sinfulness of Adam and Eve and the sinfulness of Cain? Discuss this as a whole group and reflect on Dr. Kalas' comments about grace. When did God shower Adam and Eve and Cain with grace? From the very beginning, yes. But when else? That grace is evident in God's mark of protection upon Cain. This is God's unlimited grace; this is God's reconciliation with the sinner; this is God's forgiveness of all.

As a whole group, discuss some of the reasons people find trusting in God's grace so difficult. Then ask the whole group to define at least one significant life lesson from these stories of the origins of sinfulness.

Live the Story

Ask each group member to jot down on a small slip of paper—for her or his eyes only!—the sinful nature that he or she struggles with most. Is it jealousy? pride? doubt? anger? Then encourage each person to write these words below that sin: "God's grace is sufficient to overcome even this in me." Encourage each group member to carry her or his slip of paper in pocket or purse and refer to it often.

Close this session with a prayer for forgiveness and grace. Then pray together the Lord's Prayer.

3. The Flood: Judgment and Promise
Genesis 4:18–9:29

Faith Focus
God responds to the recurring pattern of human sin not with revenge, but with redemptive punishment and grace.

Before the Session
Read the story of Noah and the Flood in several different translations. Read for meaning and purpose instead of focusing on details, such as how Noah could care for all those animals on a boat.

Be prepared to address the following: What is the enduring message of the story of Noah and the Flood? What was and is God trying to teach us through this story?

Claim Your Story
A key verse in this story is Genesis 6:5. Read this verse aloud; then ask the group members if they think that God sees the wickedness of humankind today. Does God see that our hearts are focused on evil continually? Then ask: Is God responding to what God sees in ways that mirror the Flood? Think of the massive destruction wrought by recent hurricanes, earthquakes, tsunamis, floods, and tornadoes. Is God responding to the evilness of humankind? Is God giving us a warning? What about the dire predictions about global warming? Is God warning all humanity that we must get right with God? Or are all these calamities just naturally occurring events about which we know so much more in our day of instant news coverage? Encourage group members to give reasons for their responses and to illustrate their responses with examples.

Enter the Bible Story
Enoch Walked With God
Dr. Kalas (the writer of the study) reviews for us the slow but inevitable drift of humankind away from God in these chapters from Genesis. But he also lifts up Enoch as one shining light, one example of someone who walked with God regardless of what everyone else was doing. Ask group members to call out the names of contemporary "Enochs" who in our day and age are walking with God despite what everyone else is doing. Group members may suggest members of the congregation; or they might recall international figures, such as Mother Teresa or Billy Graham. What happened to Enoch in his day, and what happens to the Enochs in our day? Was Enoch heeded? Are our Enochs heeded? Why, or why not?

Noah Walked With God

Dr. Kalas goes on to extol Noah as one who followed the way of God, who walked with God. And Dr. Kalas suggests that God raises up persons to do God's will even in the midst of degradation. We may not recognize this as such, but God always seems to provide a glimmer of hope just when things seem to be at their worst. Again, ask group members for examples. Two that come to mind are the miraculous landing of the airliner in the Hudson River and the rescue of the Chilean miners who had been trapped far underground for so long. As Noah demonstrated that God is still in control, events like these two and others cited by the group members affirm that God is still God—and we're not.

Doing as God Commands

Next, Dr. Kalas takes us to the building of the ark. "Noah did everything exactly as God commanded him" (Genesis 6:22). As a whole group ponder this question: Do we do everything exactly as God commands us? Do we love, do we forgive, do we reconcile, do we give, do we witness exactly as God commanded us? Why, or why not? Are we not more prone to question God or to take shortcuts rather than to do as God commanded? Are we teetering on the brink of being found wicked and evil, as the people of Noah's time were?

Symbols in the Story of Noah

The story of Noah contains a number of symbols. Ask teams of three to identify some of those symbols and to describe their meanings. Dr. Kalas writes of the symbol of the door of the ark, the forty days of rain, and the water itself. What other symbols do group members identify? Hear from some of the teams.

Sin Has Consequences

A significant insight that Dr. Kalas shares is that sin always has consequences. Forgiveness does not erase the consequences. The consequences of sin are inevitable, perhaps in the short term or perhaps in the long term. But the consequences are inevitable. Ask the teams of three to discuss this concept. Some in the teams may want to share personal examples, but no one should be forced to do so.

God Does Not Give Up on Us

A final point that Dr. Kalas makes is that God did not give up on humankind and God does not give up on us. In what ways does Noah's story demonstrate the forgiving love of Christ?

Live the Story

The story of Noah is a story of God's redemptive love, demonstrated in part through a cleansing punishment, the just consequences of sinfulness. Ask each group member to pray in silence for one who has wronged her or him and to find the courage to initiate forgiveness toward that person.

Close by praying together the Lord's Prayer.

4. Rebellion and Dispersal
Genesis 10:1–11:9

Faith Focus
As individuals and as communities and nations, the excessive exercise of human ambition, self-assertiveness, and autonomy moves us at our peril away from dependence on God and from God's desire for human community.

Before the Session
You'll notice that there is not quite so much reading for this week, but the reading is important—yes, even Genesis 10, with what seems to be an endless list of names. Read this chapter, but don't worry about pronunciations. Instead, note names with which you are already familiar.

Next comes the story of the tower of Babel. Again, the point is deriving the message God wants us to gain from it. Consider this story carefully; there is much more to it than simply explaining how different languages arose.

Claim Your Story
Read the following paragraph aloud; then ask the group members to discuss it in teams of four persons:

We live in a culture that honors ambition. We are taught that in our culture anyone can become what she or he wants to be if he or she only applies himself or herself. Thus, we may align ourselves with the people of Shinar and their ambition to build a tower to get as close to God as possible. Shouldn't we want to get close to God? Or is getting close to God trying to become more like God, to be God ourselves? If that is the case, only one of us can be "God." What then does that mean?

Hear from a few of the teams. Did most of the teams agree on their responses to this paragraph? Why, or why not?

Enter the Bible Story
Nimrod and Ambition
Dr. Kalas (the writer of the study) helps us focus on the genealogical lists in Genesis, for these lists were important for the ancient Israelites and remain important for religious Jews today. But he also points out the continuity between these names and the events that follow. Note his discussion of Nimrod. If Nimrod was a mighty hunter, then he was a man of mighty ambition. This ambition was transferred to his offspring in Shinar when they tried to build a tower that would lift them to God.

As a whole group, discuss the concept of ambition. When is ambition positive, and what makes ambition sometimes negative? Nimrod was ambitious; he never would have developed the skills to be a mighty hunter had he not been ambitious. Did his self-serving ambition "rub off" on his descendants? Did his ambition lead them astray? Give some examples of how this could happen in our day and time.

What can the group conclude about the value, use, and power of ambition?

The Power of Words

Note carefully Dr. Kalas' comments on the uniqueness of human language. A great lie perpetrated on children is the saying, "Sticks and stones may break my bones, but words will never hurt me." Words can hurt deeply. Words can heal as well as hurt; words can destroy as well as build up. And everyone knows that once a word is uttered, it cannot be taken back; it cannot be erased. Invite group members to respond to Dr. Kalas' careful description of the power of speech and language. Some group members might like to bear witness to the power of words in their own life stories.

Why the Desire to Build Towers?

Form four teams. Ask each team to consider these questions: Using the biblical text and Dr. Kalas' comments in this chapter of the study, why did the people of Babel want to build a tower? What were they saying about themselves in this desire? What were they saying about their future? Was the desire to build the tower in and of itself evil? If not, what made it so evil that God prevented it?

Now move to the personal: When and how do we try to build "towers" that will reach to God? When do we try to set ourselves alongside God, in the same place where God is? How did God respond to the attempt to build the tower in Babel? How does God respond to our attempt to build our "towers" to be like God?

Hear brief reports from the teams, and help them recognize (if they have not already) that we face the same kind of inability to communicate clearly when each of us insists on having her or his own way. In doing so, we set ourselves up as little gods with total disregard for those around us. This is part of the sin of the tower of Babel.

Live the Story

Ask group members to bow in silence and to respond silently to these statements as you read them aloud:

Lord, I have let my ambition rule me, blinding me to your way. Forgive me.

Lord, I have tried to be my own god, to be in charge of my own life. Forgive me.

Lord, I have neglected others and their needs, desires, and hopes. Forgive me.

Lord, I have used words to hurt, to belittle, to destroy. Forgive me.

Lord, I need to realign myself with you, for you alone are my Lord and my God.

Amen.

5. Abraham and the Turn of History
Genesis 11:10–23:20

Faith Focus

God enters into covenantal relationships with particular people in particular times and places in order to overcome the alienation between all people and God and between peoples for God's expressed purpose of bringing blessings to all.

Before the Session

Do you have access to a good Bible dictionary (perhaps in your church library or in your pastor's library)? If so, look up Abraham and learn all you can about him. The chapters about Abraham that are covered in this session can be daunting; a good Bible dictionary can summarize much of this and give you good insight into Abraham.

If no Bible dictionary is available, try this: Can you outline Abraham's life? Make a list of the major events in his life from his introduction as Abram in Genesis 11:26. You'll notice that some of these events seem to overlap or to be repeated in part. This has led some scholars to suggest that Genesis is a compilation of several ancient stories that have been woven together.

Decide whether to write the closing prayer on a chalkboard or large sheet of paper or to make copies for each group member.

Claim Your Story

Ask group members for general reactions to the Abraham story that they have read in their Bibles. Help group members recognize that Abraham's life did not flow in a straight line, anymore than our lives flow in a straight line. Abraham, like each of us, had his "ups and downs," his moments of great faithfulness and his times of faithlessness. You might ask several group members to share their own stories quickly to demonstrate again that lives do not necessarily proceed in neat, straight lines. This means that Abraham was a real person, much like each of us. True, he is regarded as a biblical superhero; but his life's trajectory was anything but direct.

Enter the Bible Story
Abraham as Both Exemplar and Flawed

Ask the whole group to consider for a moment why God chose a flawed human being for the great responsibility of being a blessing to all nations. Could not God have sent an angel to do this? After all, angels appear several times in the Abraham cycle. So why did God chose an ordinary person, an elderly person by the counting of the time, a person with no offspring, a person who possibly had flaws in his past and certainly had flaws in his future, to be such a significant spokesperson for God? Do not expect a neat, precise answer; God's ways are mysterious to us.

A question to be discussed in pairs: Did God know that Abraham would obey, even as Noah had obeyed? Was the demand made of Abraham by God any more or any less difficult than the demand made of Noah?

Notice in the biblical text and in the study the ways in which Abraham vacillates between that which is noble and good and that which is, to put it bluntly, shoddy. Abraham tricks Pharaoh by lying about his wife, then in the next scene gives his nephew first choice of the land, a choice that was rightly his as the elder. What is Abraham? Again, very, very human.

Three Dimensions of the Life of Abraham

Divide your group into three teams, and assign each team a dimension in the life of Abraham.

Team One can focus on the announcement that Sarah would conceive, the birth of Ishmael, the birth of Isaac, and the expulsion of Hagar and Ishmael. What image or picture of Abraham comes through these events? Where is God in these events? Is the text trying to teach us something here? If so, what?

Team Two might focus on the Sodom and Gomorrah cycle. Again, angels appear. Abraham bargains with God. God's justice is carried out on the wicked cities. What picture of Abraham emerges from this cycle? What is the biblical text telling us to be and to do in our time?

Team Three might focus on Genesis 22, the account of the binding of Isaac. Again, what picture of Abraham—and Isaac—emerges from this story? Recognize that this was a very difficult situation with no simple explanation. But believers must wrestle with it. What does the biblical text lead us to learn from this episode? Again, be careful: Our own histories tells us that God does not always provide a "ram caught by its horns in the dense underbrush" (Genesis 22:13) to rescue us from terrible situations.

Hear brief reports from each of the teams; but do not expect precise, complete answers. Allow the whole group to raise questions regarding each team's presentation.

Again, what is the prevailing learning to be gained from this Abraham cycle?

Live the Story

Ask the group members to join you in the following prayer. Copy the prayer on a chalkboard or large sheet of paper, or distribute copies.

Almighty God, like Abraham, I am inconsistent in my obedience to you. I question your judgment, and I fail to believe and live upon your promises. Like Abraham, I want to believe, I want to obey. But I am weak. Forgive me; and as you did with Abraham, give me another and another opportunity to be obedient to your will for me. I offer this prayer in Christ's name. Amen.

6. Isaac: A Sacred Interlude
Genesis 24:1–28:9

Faith Focus
Human and divine actions are always intertwined. God's surprising grace works through complex and sometimes self-centered human motives and behaviors to fulfill the divine purposes.

Before the Session
The story gets a bit confusing here, for a number of characters enter the stage and play significant parts. Sketch out a family tree of Abraham. See where Lot, Sarah, Hagar, Ishmael, Isaac, Rebekah, Jacob, and Esau fit. Enlarge your sketch of the family tree, and post it in your classroom so your group members can visualize this web of relationships. If your class sessions provide enough time, you might develop this family tree on a chalkboard or large sheet of paper, with the whole group contributing to it.

Claim Your Story
This session's biblical text deals with two common realities. One is, How does one choose a mate for life? The other is the reality of sibling rivalry. Divide the whole group into two teams. Have one team discuss the contemporary process for choosing a mate and the other team talk about sibling rivalry in our day and age.

Suggest that the team discussing the means of choosing a mate focus on the ways mates are chosen today. Team members may recognize that not all cultures in our day go about choosing a life's mate in the same ways. Arranged marriages are still standard in some cultures in our world.

The team members discussing sibling rivalry may discuss this concept out of their own experiences. Ask: Is sibling rivalry always negative, or can it be positive? Give examples and reasons for responding as you do. How can negative sibling rivalry be turned positive? What might cause healthy sibling rivalry to turn unhealthy?

Hear very brief reports from each of the teams, and challenge each team to reconsider some of their ideas once the whole group has studied today's Scripture.

Enter the Bible Story
Isaac as an In-between Character
The biblical text for this session begins with Isaac. Dr. Kalas (the writer of the study) suggests that Isaac is more often acted upon that than acting. He is the recipient of other people's actions rather than the initiator of actions on his own.

Invite the whole group to reflect on this observation. Does the group think that Dr. Kalas is on target with this appraisal? Or do some in the group feel that

Isaac is being sold short by this characterization? Encourage the group members to give reasons for responding as they do.

Dr. Kalas suggests that Isaac is an in-between character, in between the two strong characters of Abraham and Jacob. As a whole group, ponder this question: Could Jacob have followed immediately after Abraham? If the group thinks not, what part did Isaac play in this drama of God working with humankind?

Isaac and Rebekah's Sons

A second set of questions concerns Isaac and Rebekah's children. Again, these children were almost miraculous. Like Sarah, Rebekah appeared to be barren. Only through prayer—and at an advanced age—did Rebekah conceive. How soon did she know that she was to bear fraternal twins? We simply do not know. But her faith led her to trust in God.

Again as a whole group, consider several questions related to the birth of the twins: What was God saying to Isaac and Rebekah—and what is God saying to us—through the birth of these twins? What lessons are we to learn? The twins were fraternal, not identical; and the Scriptures report that they were very different in personality, stature, and interests. The implication is that Isaac favored Esau while Rebekah favored the stay-at-home boy, Jacob. Do parents naturally favor one child over another, or was this a flaw in the character of Isaac and Rebekah? Give reasons for your answer.

Jacob's Cheating of Esau

Again as a whole group, consider Jacob's outright cheating of Esau. What is the group's reaction to the exchange of a birthright for a pot of stew? What is the group's reaction to the lies and trickery involved in hoodwinking Isaac into giving Jacob the blessing that belonged to Esau?

And again, what does this entire saga teach us about God's ways with God's creation? Whom does God choose to do God's work in the world? What is God choosing the group members to do and to be for God?

Live the Story

Invite the group members to a time of confession and prayer. Remind the group members that nearly all of us have lied, cheated, and perhaps taken advantage of another person. Invite the group to a time of silent prayer in which each can recall and confess such acts in silence. End the time of silent prayer by reminding the group members that they are indeed forgiven by the grace of God and that God still has work for them to do.

7. Jacob: The Making of a Patriarch
Genesis 28:10–36:8

Faith Focus

God promises to be with us—through times of inspiration, hard work, disappointment, struggle, anxiety, and danger—sustaining us and drawing us into the divine plan.

Before the Session

Recall from the last session that Jacob had tricked Esau—twice!—and now feared for his life. So Jacob, the consummate trickster and rogue, with orders to marry one of his kinswomen rather than a Canaanite woman, runs for his life. His fear of Esau is deep and real. After all, he had connived to cheat Esau out of almost everything that he had. Did Jacob learn his lesson?

Read these chapters with the understanding that Jacob was a human being who had character flaws. Again, God was using the most unlikely of persons to do God's will!

Claim Your Story

Invite group members to consider the sweep of Jacob's story from these chapters. Ask: Was Jacob's life a straight line or a line with many twists and turns in it? Was Jacob always obedient to God? If not, to what was Jacob obedient?

Then, in teams of three, consider these questions: Have our lives been straight lines, or have they been filled with turns and twists? Some in the teams might like to give illustrations of their answers. Have we always been obedient to God? If not, to whom or to what have we been obedient?

Enter the Bible Story
Jacob Meets God

So Jacob ran. He ran from home and family. He ran toward relatives in the hope that he would be welcomed there. He wearied, so he stretched out to rest and sleep.

And Jacob had a dream.

Invite the group to form teams of four. Then read aloud Genesis 28:10-17. Ask the teams of four to discuss this reading with these questions in mind: In this dream, where was Jacob? Where was God? What symbolic purpose did the ladder serve? Was the ladder there so that Jacob might climb to heaven or so that Jacob could recognize that God had come to earth? Help the group members recognize that this passage is incarnational; it is an early example of *Immanuel*, God is with us. In a way, the popular song "We Are Climbing Jacob's Ladder" misses the point. The ladder is a symbol of God coming down to us, not Jacob's—or our—attempt to go up to God.

Ask group members to read silently Dr. Kalas' (the study writer's) insightful comments on Jacob's dream and what followed immediately. Notice, as Dr. Kalas points out, that Jacob could not resist trying to strike a deal with God, even in this high and holy moment.

Jacob Finds a New Family

Invite group members to refer to the study to identify the main characters in this story. Jacob is central, but so is Laban. The two sisters, Rachel and Leah, are not central to the action. The two maids, Bilhah and Zilpah, also emerge in the story; but like Rachel and Leah, they are not dominant actors.

Thus, the two central actors seem to be Jacob and Laban. Set up a dialogue between "Jacob" and "Laban" by asking two group members to roleplay these parts. Let the actors make up their lines as they go along. First, roleplay the conversation between Jacob and Laban when Jacob asks for Rachel. Laban strikes a hard bargain. The seven years pass quickly. Now roleplay the conversation between Jacob and Laban when Jacob discovers he was tricked and had married Leah instead of Rachel. Finally, roleplay a possible dialogue between Laban and Jacob over the speckled, spotted, and black lambs. Again, the trickery is paramount, each man trying to outdo the other.

After the roleplays, ask this question for comment by the whole group: Where is God in all this?

Jacob Meets God, and Esau

The third emphasis made by Dr. Kalas is Jacob's encounter with Esau—and with an angel—in a wrestling match. In teams of three, focus on these events through these questions: What do you think of Jacob's attempt to appease Esau with gifts? What is your reaction to Jacob's willingness to send his family and all his flocks across the river to confront Esau while he, Jacob, stayed on the safe side of the river?

Dr. Kalas offers several suggestions as to who the stranger was who wrestled with Jacob. Who do you think the stranger was, or whom did the stranger symbolize or represent? Do you think Jacob was changed as a result of this encounter?

Live the Story

As Dr. Kalas points out, Esau, the offended brother, was the brother who extended forgiveness and grace. Invite the group members to reflect in silence on those times when they have been recipients of unexpected grace and forgiveness. What was going on in Esau's life that he could forgive so completely? What must go on in our lives in order to be able to do the same?

Encourage each group member to offer a silent prayer for the courage to initiate reconciliation with one who has offended her or him.

8. Joseph's Place in the Big Story
Genesis 37–50

Faith Focus
The story of Joseph witnesses to the providence of God: God's ability and determination to bring good even out of evil.

Before the Session
The Scripture for this session is extensive, but it reads like a popular story. It is a story of arrogance; betrayal; injustice; success; and, in the end, a kind of salvation. As you read this engaging story, watch continually for the action and activity of God, both externally in events and internally within Joseph. As you have with other biblical characters in Genesis, so try to do with Joseph: What was God saying in and through Joseph, and what is God's message for us today in the story of Joseph?

Claim Your Story
Joseph finds himself in this story in deep trouble, usually through no fault of his own. True, his youthful arrogance was off-putting to his brothers; but their reaction far exceeded that which was necessary. Joseph was then imprisoned unjustly. He had tried to do the right thing; and because he did, he was thrown into jail. Thus, the Joseph story is a story of triumph over great tribulations. Ask the group to form teams of four persons each and discuss together stories of triumph over great tribulations (either in the lives of the team members or in the lives of other persons known to the team members). Ask the teams to reflect on these stories. What is the common thread that seems to run through each? What turns trials into triumphs?

Enter the Bible Story
Joseph's Unique Relationship to Jacob and the Brothers Get Revenge
Joseph was his father's favorite. But note Dr. Kalas' suggested reason why this was so. By his old age, Jacob had left his life of trickery and deception and settled into a quiet life of trust in God. Thus, he could identify Joseph as his spiritual heir if not necessarily his legal heir (the status of the firstborn son). Discuss this situation as a whole group. Was Jacob being fair with his sons? Did Joseph display an early sensitivity to the things of God that Jacob recognized and nurtured? Ask some of the "younger sons" in your group what feelings they might have had regarding their place in the birth order.

But what about that coat? Was Joseph goading his brothers by wearing such a garment to the pasture? And what about those dreams of his ascendancy over his brothers? Was this also a goading gesture on his part? What do group members think?

Set up a roleplay depicting some of the brothers and Joseph out in the field. The brothers plot, Joseph protests, Reuben and Judah intervene, and the brothers strike a deal with the Midianites. Don't necessarily follow the wording in the biblical text; let the roleplayers choose and use their own words. Dr. Kalas suggests that Judah was a bit of a hero in this episode. What do group members think?

Joseph as Slave, Prisoner, and Prime Minister

So Joseph was sold as a slave. How would group members describe Joseph's feelings at this point? List some of the emotions that must have run through Joseph at this time. Did he feel anger, despair, frustration, hopelessness—what? As group members are listing these feelings, invite them to discuss some of the reasons Joseph rose so quickly to a place of responsibility, both in Potiphar's house and in the prison.

Joseph was imprisoned on totally false charges. Can group members recall times they have suffered for trying to do the right thing? But again, Joseph rose to the occasion and was placed in charge of the prison. Ponder: What gave Joseph the power or insight to interpret the dreams of the steward and the baker? What gave Joseph the power later to interpret the dreams of the pharaoh? Regardless, Joseph quickly rose to a position of second only to Pharaoh in Egypt.

Joseph as Son and Sibling

Again, try some roleplay. The brothers approach Joseph, needing food due to the famine. Joseph toys with them. Act it out. Then Joseph finally relents and reveals himself to his brothers, not in anger, but in grace and forgiveness. Roleplay this scene as well.

Raise these questions for discussion by the whole group: What made Joseph so successful? If the group members answer that God was with him—and God was—then do the group members see the entire lifetime of Joseph as part of God's plan? Might God have similar plans for us today, plans that involve hardship and trials as well as successes? Give reasons for answering as you do.

Live the Story

Your group has considered one of the basic books of the Bible. But simply knowing the wonderful stories of Genesis is not enough. Ask group members to call out significant learnings they have acquired from their study of Genesis. What do they know about God now that they did not know before they participated in this study? What have they learned about the ways God works with God's people? And just who are God's people?

Ask each group member to reflect in silence on how her or his life has been changed through this study. Then pray together the Lord's Prayer.